IPSAS Explained

IPSAS Explained

A Summary of International
Public Sector Accounting Standards

Thomas Müller-Marqués Berger

WILEY

A John Wiley and Sons, Ltd, Publication

Quality In Everything We Do

Foreword

In many countries all over the world, public sector accounting is in a phase of transition to resource-oriented, accrual-based accounting. Both nationally and internationally, however, considerable differences between the accounting systems and the published financial statements can be identified. Accordingly, public sector accounting is highly diversified, in formal respects and also with regard to the content. These developments are moving away from the key objectives of public management, which include reducing bureaucracy, achieving comparable standards in terms of accountability and transparency. Debates in recent years and developments in France or Switzerland, for example, have shown that the International Public Sector Accounting Standards (IPSASs) could be a suitable means of harmonizing and aligning public sector accounting.

As a global organization with a strong focus on the public sector, Ernst & Young has therefore set about offering a contribution to the further development and harmonization of public sector accounting. This publication is intended to provide decision-makers in the public sector with an overview of the IPSASs and the International Public Sector Accounting Standards Board (IPSASB). Each IPSAS is presented in brief in the following, focusing on the core content of the relevant standard. In the interest of readability, we decided in most cases not to look at the – often extensive – disclosures in the notes required by the IPSASs.

This book is based on the IPSASs and Exposure Drafts (EDs) as at 1 July 2009.

If you have any comments or suggestions, we would be happy to consider them for a second edition of this publication. Please send an e-mail to thomas.mueller-marques.berger@de.ey.com. We would like to thank everyone who has contributed to this publication for their valuable support. A special thank you goes to Dr. Jens Heiling, Dr. Holger Wirtz and Karin Viehmann for their outstanding level of commitment.

Thomas Müller-Marqués Berger, Stuttgart, July 2009

Contents

Contents

VIII

Abbreviations

ADB	Asian Development Bank, Manila
approx.	Approximately
CICA	Canadian Institute of Chartered Accountants, Toronto
e.g.	*exempli gratia*, for example
EC	European Commission, Brussels
ED	Exposure Draft
ed.	Edition
Et seq.	*et sequens/et sequentes*, and the following one(s)
EU	European Union
FIFO	First-in, first-out inventory valuation method
GBE	Government Business Enterprises
GGS	General government sector
i.e.	*id est*, that is
IAS	International Accounting Standard
IASB	International Accounting Standards Board, London
IFAC	International Federation of Accountants, New York
IFRIC	International Financial Reporting Interpretations Committee
IFRS	International Financial Reporting Standard
IMF	International Monetary Fund, Washington, D.C.
INTOSAI	International Organization of Supreme Audit Institutions, Vienna
IPSAS	International Public Sector Accounting Standard
IPSASB	International Public Sector Accounting Standards Board, New York
ISA	International Standards on Auditing
n/a	not applicable
NATO	North Atlantic Treaty Organization, Brussels
OECD	Organisation for Economic Co-operation and Development, Paris
p.	Page
PAP	Project Advisory Panel
para.	Paragraph
PFCS	Public Financial Corporations Sector
PNFCS	Public Non-Financial Corporations Sector
PSC	Public Sector Committee
SC	Steering Committee
SECO	State Secretariat for Economic Affairs, Berne
SIC	Standing Interpretations Committee

SNA	System of National Accounts
UK ASB	United Kingdom Accounting Standards Board, London
UN	United Nations, New York
UNDP	United Nations Development Program
UNESCO	United Nations Educational, Scientific and Cultural Organisation, Paris
UNICEF	United Nation International Children Emergency Fund, New York
WFP	World Food Program, Rome

I Introduction: General information about IPSASs and the IPSASB

1 The International Public Sector Accounting Standards Board (IPSASB)

1.1 General information

The International Public Sector Accounting Standards – IPSASs for short – govern the accounting by public sector entities, with the exception of Government Business Enterprises. According to the IPSASB regulations, Government Business Enterprises should apply the International Financial Reporting Standards (IFRSs) issued by the IASB, as do private sector entities. IPSASs are developed by the International Public Sector Accounting Standards Board (IPSASB). It is an independent board founded by the International Federation of Accountants (IFAC) to develop and publish IPSASs.

The IFAC is an international organization for the accountancy profession. It was founded in 1977 and is domiciled in New York. According to the bylaws of the International Federation of Accountants, its mission is as follows: "to serve the public interest, IFAC will continue to strengthen the worldwide accountancy profession and contribute to the development of strong international economies by establishing and promoting adherence to high-quality professional standards, furthering the international convergence of such standards and speaking out on public interest issues where the profession's expertise is most relevant." The IFAC had this in mind when it established the Public Sector Committee (PSC) in 1986 as a standing technical committee. The PSC initially focused on preparing and publishing studies and research reports on (international) public sector accounting. In 2004, the PSC was renamed IPSASB.

1.2 Structure and organization of the IPSASB

The members of the IPSASB are appointed based on recommendations by a nominating committee of the IFAC. The appointments are then made by the IFAC, considering technical and professional criteria, as well as a geographic and gender balance.

The chart below shows the structure and organization of the IPSASB:

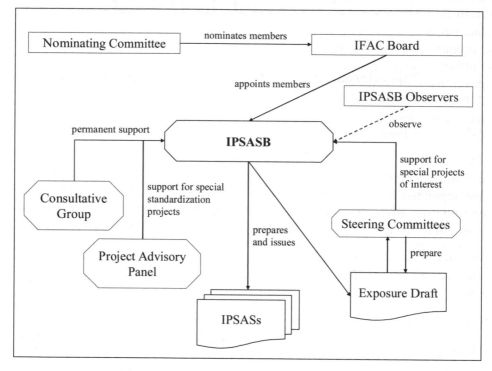

Figure 1: Structure and organization of the IPSASB

The primary objective of the IPSASB is to develop IPSASs and issue pronouncements. The IPSASB may delegate responsibility for conducting the necessary research and drafting of proposed standards and guidance or draft surveys to steering committees, subcommittees, individuals or staff. In each case, these committees are chaired by a member of the IPSASB, but they can include non-members of the IPSASB or the IFAC. The work of these committees is usually issued in the form of exposure drafts, which are made available to the general public. The publication of exposure drafts is intended to give interested individuals or groups the opportunity to submit comments (usually three to four months or more). This allows the groups concerned by IPSASs to voice their opinion before the standards are adopted and published by the IPSASB. The observers of the IPSASB include organizations that have an interest in public sector financial reporting, such as the European Union (EU), the International Monetary Fund (IMF), the Organisation for Economic Co-operation and Development (OECD) or the World Bank. As their role is of a supervisory nature, they are not entitled to vote.

Besides financial support from the IFAC, the IPSASB also receives funding from external sources. The IPSASB enjoys significant financial support from international organizations such as the Asian Development Bank (ADB), the European Commission (EC), the United Nations (UN) and the World Bank. Further financial resources are provided by the government of Canada, the government of New Zealand and Switzerland's State Secretariat for Economic Affairs (SECO). Personnel support is available to the IPSASB in the form of technical consultants provided by the People's Republic of China and the Canadian Institute of Chartered Accountants (CICA).

The consultative group of the IPSASB provides a platform to facilitate the exchange of information between the IPSASB and specialists. Its members are appointed by the IPSASB. The IPSASB chair also acts as chair of the consultative group. The consultative group is above all a virtual forum and does not have voting rights.

In addition to IPSASs, the IPSASB issues other, non-binding publications such as studies, research reports and occasionally discussion papers dealing with specific accounting issues for the public sector.

1.3 Objectives of the IPSASB

The objective of the IPSASB is to serve the public interest by developing high-quality accounting standards for the public sector and by facilitating the convergence of international and national standards, thereby enhancing the quality and standardization of financial reporting around the world. Public interest in the pronouncement of IPSASs may arise, for example, from a national or supranational need to harmonize financial reporting of public sector entities. It is also in the public interest to continue developing public sector accounting by means of the IPSASB standardization projects. The IPSASB achieves these goals by:

- Publishing International Public Sector Accounting Standards (IPSASs)
- Promoting their acceptance and compliance on an international scale with these standards
- Publishing other documents that contain guidance on issues and experience with financial reporting in the public sector

1.4 Members of the IPSASB

The members of the IPSASB are appointed by the IFAC Board. The IPSASB comprises a total of 18 members, 15 of whom are nominated by member organizations of the IFAC. The other three are public members, who can be nominated by any individual or organization. All IPSASB meetings convened to develop IPSASs or approve their publication are public.

The table below shows the countries represented on the IPSASB:

▪ United Kingdom (chair)	▪ Germany	▪ Netherlands
▪ Australia	▪ India	▪ New Zealand
▪ Canada	▪ Israel	▪ South Africa
▪ China	▪ Japan	▪ Turkey*
▪ France	▪ Kenya	▪ United States of America

Table 1:   Members of the IPSASB (without public members) (as of January 2009)
*   * The Turkish member was expelled from the IPSASB in 2009.*

In addition, the IPSASB appoints a limited number of observers from organizations that have an interest in public sector financial reporting. These observers have full rights of the floor at IPSASB meetings, but no voting rights. The list below shows the organizations that have observer status:

- Asian Development Bank (ADB)
- European Union (EU)
- Eurostat
- International Accounting Standards Board (IASB)
- International Monetary Fund (IMF)
- International Organisation of Supreme Audit Institutions (INTOSAI)
- Organization for Economic Co-operation and Development (OECD)
- United Nations Development Programme (UN/UNDP)
- World Bank

Table 2:   Organizations with observer status on the IPSASB (as of July 2009)

2   International accounting standards for the public sector

2.1   Overview of international accounting standards for the public sector

The IPSASB develops IPSASs for financial statements prepared on the accrual basis of accounting as well as for financial statements prepared on the cash basis of accounting. IPSASs govern the recognition, measurement, presentation and disclosure requirements in relation to transactions and events in **general purpose financial statements**. Such financial statements are characterized by the fact that they are issued for users who are unable to demand financial information to meet their specific information needs.

With respect to the development of the IPSASs on the accrual basis of accounting, the IPSASB pursues the aim of convergence of IPSASs and IFRSs. The International Financial Reporting Standards (IFRSs) are therefore used as a starting point for developing new IPSASs. The IPSASB will adapt IFRSs only if the public sector has specific accounting requirements. Provided these specific requirements of the public sector are taken into account, the IPSASB seeks to retain the accounting treatment and original text of the IFRSs. The specific requirements of the public sector, such as transactions without consideration (e.g., taxes and transfers) or public fund management, however mean that the IPSASB does issue accounting standards for which there is no corresponding IFRS. These IPSASs principally contain rules not dealt with, or only to a minor extent, by existing IFRSs. The table below provides an overview of the international accounting standards for the public sector (as of 1 July 2009) and the underlying IFRSs:

IPSAS	Title	Correspon-ding IFRS
IPSAS 1	Presentation of Financial Statements	IAS 1
IPSAS 2	Cash Flow Statements	IAS 7
IPSAS 3	Accounting Policies, Changes in Accounting Estimates and Errors	IAS 8
IPSAS 4	The Effects of Changes in Foreign Exchange Rates	IAS 21
IPSAS 5	Borrowing Costs	IAS 23
IPSAS 6	Consolidated and Separate Financial Statements	IAS 27
IPSAS 7	Investments in Associates	IAS 28
IPSAS 8	Interests in Joint Ventures	IAS 31
IPSAS 9	Revenue from Exchange Transactions	IAS 18
IPSAS 10	Financial Reporting in Hyperinflationary Economies	IAS 29
IPSAS 11	Construction Contracts	IAS 11
IPSAS 12	Inventories	IAS 2
IPSAS 13	Leases	IAS 17
IPSAS 14	Events After the Reporting Date	IAS 10
IPSAS 15	Financial Instruments: Disclosure and Presentation	IAS 32
IPSAS 16	Investment Property	IAS 40
IPSAS 17	Property, Plant and Equipment	IAS 16
IPSAS 18	Segment Reporting	IAS 14
IPSAS 19	Provisions, Contingent Liabilities and Contingent Assets	IAS 37

IPSAS 20	Related Party Disclosures	IAS 24
IPSAS 21	Impairment of Non-Cash-Generating Assets	No directly corresponding IFRS
IPSAS 22	Disclosure of Financial Information about the General Government Sector	No corresponding IFRS
IPSAS 23	Revenue from Non-Exchange Transactions (Taxes and Transfers)	No corresponding IFRS
IPSAS 24	Presentation of Budget Information in Financial Statements	No corresponding IFRS
IPSAS 25	Employee Benefits	IAS 19
IPSAS 26	Impairment of Cash-Generating Assets	IAS 36
Cash Basis IPSAS	Cash Basis IPSAS: Financial Reporting Under the Cash Basis of Accounting	No corresponding IFRS

Table 3: Overview of the international accounting standards for the public sector (as of 1 July 2009)

The following table gives an overview of the Proposed International Public Sector Accounting Standards (Exposure Drafts) as of 1 July 2009:

Exposure Draft (ED)	Title	Corresponding IFRS
ED 36	Agriculture	IAS 41
ED 37	Financial Instruments: Presentation	IAS 32
ED 38	Financial Instruments: Recognition and Measurement	IAS 39
ED 39	Financial Instruments: Disclosures	IFRS 7
ED 40	Intangible Assets	IAS 38
ED 41	Entity Combinations from Exchange Transactions	IFRS 3
ED 42	Improvements to IPSASs	n/a

Table 4: Overview of the Proposed International Public Sector Accounting Standards (Exposure Drafts) as of 1 July 2009

2.2　History of the International Public Sector Accounting Standards

The IPSASs are based on the work of the PSC of the IFAC. This standing committee has been dealing with public sector accounting and audits since 1986. Its core tasks include the development of concepts to optimize the financial management and financial reporting of public authorities. In its early days, the PSC developed and promulgated a large number of guidelines, studies and research reports. However, these pronouncements did not play such an important role as IPSASs today.

The Standards Project launched in 1996 marked a turning point in the work of the PSC. The purpose of the Standards Project was to formulate IPSASs aimed at improving the financial management and accounting of public authorities and harmonizing public accounting at an international level. This project fundamentally changed the way the PSC saw itself; from then on it considered itself an independent committee for the standardization of public sector accounting and changed its name to IPSASB in 2004.

2.3　Scope of the International Public Sector Accounting Standards

IPSASs are intended for application for **general purpose financial statements** of all public sector entities. Public sector entities generally include national and regional governments (e.g., state, provincial, territorial governments), local authorities (e.g., towns and cities) as well as related governmental entities (e.g., agencies, boards, commissions and enterprises). As already mentioned, IPSASs do not apply to **Government Business Enterprises**.

A Government Business Enterprise within the meaning of IPSASs is an entity that has all of the following characteristics:

1.　It is an entity with the power to contract in its own name.
2.　It has been assigned the financial and operational authority to carry on a business.
3.　It sells goods and services, in the normal course of its business, to other entities at profit or full cost recovery.
4.　It is not reliant on continuing government funding to be a going concern (other than purchases of outputs at arm's length).
5.　It is controlled by a public sector entity.

The characteristics of Government Business Enterprises show that within the meaning of IPSASs these entities operate on an economically sustainable basis, i.e., they must at least cover their costs or have the intention of

7

generating a profit. Typically, they are controlled or owned by state, regional or local government.

2.4   General purpose financial statements

Financial statements that are issued for users who are not in a position to demand financial information to meet their specific information needs are referred to as **general purpose financial statements**. Examples of such users of financial statements are citizens, voters, their political representatives and other members of the general public. The term "financial statements" used here and in the standards covers all disclosures and notes that have been identified as components of the general purpose financial statements.

Financial statements prepared on the accrual basis of accounting comprise a statement of financial position, a statement of financial performance, a cash flow statement and a statement of changes in net assets/equity. For financial statements prepared on the cash basis of accounting, the statement of cash receipts and payments is the primary component.

In addition to the general purpose financial statements a public sector entity may prepare financial statements for other parties (such as executive committees, the legislature and other parties with supervisory functions) that can request financial information tailored to their needs. Such financial statements are referred to as **special purpose financial statements**. The IPSASB recommends that IPSASs also be adopted for special purpose financial statements where appropriate.

2.5   Authority of the International Public Sector Accounting Standards

The IPSASB recognizes the right of governments and national standard setters to establish accounting standards and associated guidance within their jurisdictions. Its objectives are "to serve the public interest by developing high-quality public sector financial reporting standards and by facilitating the convergence of international and national standards, thereby enhancing the quality and uniformity of financial reporting throughout the world". Thus, the IPSASB sees itself in a supportive function. The general purpose financial statements of public sector entities may be governed by rules or laws in a jurisdiction. These rules may take the form of statutory reporting rules, directives or statements on accounting and/or accounting standards issued by governments, regulatory authorities and/or professional associations in the jurisdiction.

However, neither the IPSASB nor the accounting and audit profession can enforce compliance with IPSASs on their own. This means that IPSASs do not have a directly binding effect for territorial authorities or other public sector entities.

The existing IPSASs can assist legislators and national standard setters in developing new standards or revising existing ones in order to achieve greater comparability of public sector entities' financial statements at a national and international level. The IPSASs can be of great help especially for all jurisdictions that do not have accrual basis accounting standards for the public sector yet.

Developing countries are one of the main target groups for IPSASs. Financial institutions such as the Asian Development Bank, the International Monetary Fund or the World Bank play an important role as major donors and lending institutions for these countries. The strategy of providing financial resources to developing countries via these institutions nowadays is mostly focused on creating transparent and consistent financial reporting structures as a basis for further financial help in the future. Accordingly, financial aid by these institutions is often related to the implementation of reporting procedures and structures based on IPSASs. For example, the World Bank encourages borrowers to prepare their financial reports in accordance with IPSASs. Thus, the IPSASs are gaining in importance as an internationally accepted standard.

However, in the so-called developed part of the world there is also an increasing demand for the adoption of IPSASs for compatibility and comparability reasons. The various processes of collection and reallocation of resources employed by different countries, such as within the European Union, create the need for transparency regarding allocation criteria and the use of these means – especially in times of limited financial resources.

Given that IPSASs are the only internationally accepted public sector accounting model, these standards therefore are a guideline for the new member states in the eastern part of Europe who have decided to establish a state-of-the-art accounting system following the destruction of the old political systems.

But also in established European countries like Austria, France and Germany, the need to modernize budgeting and financial reporting systems is uncontested. The IPSASs are regarded as a reference model for the reform of governmental accounting there.

The IPSASB strongly recommends adopting IPSASs and harmonizing national requirements of public sector accounting and financial reporting with

9

those of IPSASs. Some states and national standard setters have already developed generally accepted accounting standards for the public sector in their jurisdiction. In many jurisdictions, however, public sector accounting is still highly fragmented, typically containing special rules for certain levels or areas.

The IPSASB believes that the application of IPSASs, together with a statement of compliance, significantly enhances the quality of general purpose financial statements prepared by public sector entities. In turn, this improves the basis for decisions on the appropriation of funds by public authorities, allowing for greater transparency and accountability.

2.6   Strategy of the IPSASB and actual projects

The **strategy of the IPSASB** for the development of standards for the public sector can be broken down into different working periods or stages of maturity of the board:

- First working period: Creation of a core set of standards

- Second working period: Transition period

- Third working period: Further development of public-sector-specific issues

During the first period, the main target of the board was the creation of a core set of IPSASs based on IFRS. Thereby, the IPSASB was able to build on an accounting basis that was well established in the private sector. The first period took place between 1996 and 2002. IPSAS 1 to IPSAS 20 (the so-called "core set of accounting standards for the public sector") were developed during this period.

The IPSASB is currently in the second phase, which is a kind of transition period. The aim of this period is, on the one hand, to reach full convergence of the IPSAS standards with the IFRSs as approved by 31 December 2008 – either by adjusting existing standards or by closing gaps through developing new ones. The IPSASB's goal is to realize a stable platform date for all second generation IPSASs by 1 January 2010 (to take effect for periods commencing on or after 1 January 2011).

On the other hand, public sector issues are coming to the fore and consequently public-sector-specific standard setting is more focussed. IPSAS 22 "Disclosure of Financial Information about the General Government Sector", IPSAS 23 "Revenue from Non-Exchange Transactions (Taxes and Transfers)" and IPSAS 24 "Presentation of Budget Information in

Financial Statements" consider the specific requirements of the public sector with regard to accounting and financial reporting. The process for reviewing and modifying IASB documents (as described below) reflects the rationale of the IPSASB of differentiating between a convergence project, i.e., adapting an IFRS to the public sector, and a public-sector-specific project for developing a new standard.

In the third part of the strategy, the aim of the board will be to detach itself further from the work of the IASB and to focus on providing answers to accounting and financial reporting issues that are unique to the public sector. The creation of an unparalleled and independent conceptual framework (see below for further details) and the decision not to await the results of the improvements project regarding the IFRS framework might be seen as bridge to that final stage of maturity of the IPSASB.

The maturity process described, and especially reaching the final development phase, is a necessary step to secure the right of existence for the board in the long run. Given the importance of the public sector for the development of societies and their welfare, it is absolutely necessary for a governmental accounting board to sharpen its profile as specialized in and focussed on the public sector.

Actual projects: In 2006 the IPSASB started a collaborative project with participation from a group of national standards setters and other organizations to develop a conceptual framework for general purpose financial reporting by public sector entities. The conceptual framework is regarded as a necessary means for ensuring coherent and consistent standards. The framework will establish the concepts applicable in developing IPSASs and other documents that provide guidance on information to be included in general purpose financial reports. The project is organized in four phases:

- **Phase 1** deals with the objectives of financial reporting, the scope of financial reporting, the qualitative characteristics of information included in general purpose financial reports and the reporting entity.
- **Phase 2** covers mainly the definition and recognition of the elements that are reported in financial statements.
- **Phase 3** considers the measurement base(s) that are adopted for the elements that are recognized in the financial statements. Presentation and disclosure under IPSAS, i.e., the nature and content of the primary financial statements and notes to the financial statements, will also be discussed.

In September 2008, the IPSASB issued the consultation paper on phase 1 of the project. In its May 2009 meeting the IPSASB reviewed the responses to the consultation paper. The main areas of the discussion were the authority of the framework and the identification of relevant users. While further analysis on phase 1 is still necessary, the IPSASB has started to discuss issues raised in phase 2 and 3. A consultation paper coming out of phase 2 is expected in late 2010.

The IPSASB has set up a project on long-term fiscal sustainability and will publish a consultation paper entitled "Long-Term Fiscal Sustainability in the Context of General Purpose Financial Reporting" by October 2009. The consultation paper provides a framework for the reporting and disclosure of information on the long-term sustainability of government programs.

As a result of self-evaluation, the IPSASB has recognized the need to simplify and align the structure and the content of the standards in the future. This should improve the readability and make adoption of the standards more attractive to preparers and other users. However, due to capacity reasons and the importance of actual standard-setting projects, a project on readability and understandability, redrafting all existing IPSASs, could not be realized by the IPSASB in the near future and was therefore postponed. Given that the complexity and the lack of readability is a point of criticism directed at IFRSs, this future project could lead to a major improvement in the history of international public accounting standard setting – and be a further step towards the IPSASB achieving a profile of its own as independent standard setter for the public sector.

2.7 Process for reviewing and modifying IASB documents

The IPSASB addresses public sector financial reporting issues in two different ways: on the one hand, the IPSASB develops public-sector-specific IPSASs which have no equivalent in IFRS. Typically, these IPSASs deal with issues that have not been comprehensively or appropriately dealt with in IFRS or for which there is no related IFRS. On the other hand, the IPSASB develops IPSASs that are converged with IFRS by adapting them to the public sector context.

In order to have guidelines for the development of IPSASs by adaptation, the IPSASB developed its "Process for Reviewing and Modifying IASB Documents" in October 2008. The IPSASB will use the analysis resulting from this process when developing the related IPSASB document to determine whether identified public sector issues warrant departures from the

IASB document. The IPSASB will use professional judgement in reaching its conclusions.

The IPSASB is using the following "Process for Reviewing and Modifying IASB Documents" for its analysis:

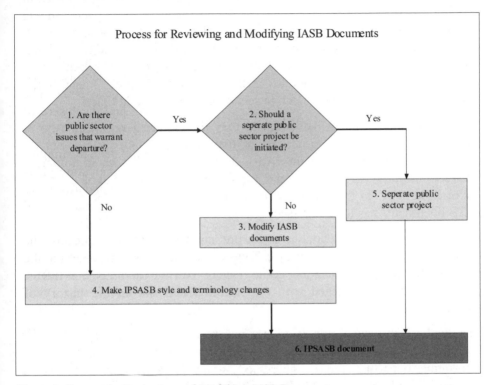

Figure 2: Process for Reviewing and Modifying IASB Documents

The goal of the first step in the analysis is to determine whether there are public sector issues that warrant a departure in recognition, measurement or in presentation or disclosure from an IASB document.

Therefore, it has to be considered whether applying the requirements of the IASB documents would mean (i) that objectives of public sector financial reporting are not adequately met, (ii) that the qualitative characteristics of public sector financial reporting are not adequately met, or (iii) that undue costs or efforts are required.

The decisions of the IPSASB are made in the context of consistency with the Conceptual Framework for General Purpose Financial Reporting by Public

Sector Entities as it develops, of internal consistency with the existing IPSASs and of consistency with the statistical bases.

In the event that identified public sector issues do not warrant departure, step 4 is applied. If identified public sector issues do warrant departure, step 2 follows.

The goal of the second step is to decide whether to initiate a separate public sector project by considering the nature of the identified public sector issue. The need to consider the nature of the identified public sector issue arises when a public sector issue is not dealt with at all in an IASB document. In this case, it is likely that a separate public sector project will be initiated.

In other situations, the IASB document may deal with an issue but may not address public sector circumstances, or may not do so adequately. For the decision whether to amend an IASB document or whether to initiate a separate public sector project (a) the importance and prevalence of the public sector issue and (b) the adequacy with which it has been dealt with in the IASB documents has to be assessed.

If step 2 leads to a separate public sector project, a project brief is prepared for the IPSASB approval and the project follows the regular standard-setting due process. If the public-sector-specific issues can be addressed within a document that is converged with the related IASB document, step 3 will apply.

The goal of the third step is to set parameters for modifying an IASB document to address public sector departures. When public sector issues warranting departure can be addressed in an IPSASB document that is converged with a related IASB document with some modification, it is important to establish parameters for the extent of modification. Modifications are made only to address the public sector issue that triggered the amendment. The IPSASB paper concerning the "Process for Reviewing and Modifying IASB Documents" lists possible modifications and/or amendments for modifying IASB documents.

The goal of the fourth step is to identify changes in style and terminology to be applied to all IPSASs. In many cases, the style and terminology of an IPSASB document that is converged with a related IASB document will require changes.

Amendments, which will be limited according to the IPSASB, could result from the following considerations:

i)   Changes in style that simplify or clarify the document from a public sector perspective.

ii)   Definitions in an IASB document that have no public sector context may be deleted.

iii) References to an IASB document for which there is no equivalent IPSAS will be replaced with the relevant international or national accounting standard dealing with that specific topic.

iv)   Terminology changes may be made to better reflect the public sector scope of the documents.

v)   Each IPSAS will be accompanied by a Basis for Conclusions that does not form part of the IPSAS. The Basis for Conclusions will focus on the modifications to the IASB document. Specifically, it will include a detailed description of the public sector issue, the rationale for departing from the related IASB document, and the implication of the changes.

vi)   Initial adoption and transitional provisions may differ to reflect public sector circumstances.

Steps 3 and 4 will give an existing IASB document a "public sector flavor". In step 5 a separate public sector project will be initiated. After reaching a conclusion, the IPSASB will apply its standard-setting due process in developing the final standard.

The process of reviewing IASB documents is ongoing and will be regularly assessed to determine whether any changes are needed to enhance the process.

2.8   Procedures for developing accounting standards

To develop IPSASs, the IPSASB has chosen a due process that gives interested parties such as the IFAC member organizations, auditors and accountants, preparers of financial statements (including ministries of finance), standard setters and individuals the opportunity to submit their comments. In addition, the IPSASB has a consultative group to discuss important projects, technical questions and priorities relating to the working program.

The IPSASB's due process for a project generally comprises the steps illustrated in figure 3:

Study of national accounting requirements and practice and an exchange of views about the issues with national standard setters

Consideration of pronouncements issued by the International Accounting standards Board (IASB), national standard setters, regulatory authorities and other authoritative bodies, professional accounting bodies, and other organizations interested in financial reporting in the public sector

Formation of steering committees (SCs), project advisory panels (PAPs) or subcommittees to provide input to the IPSASB on a project (optional)

Publication of an exposure draft for public comment usually for at least four months. This provides an opportunity for those affected by the IPSASB's pronouncements to present their views before the pronouncements are finalized and approved by the IPSASB. The exposure draft will include a basis for conclusion.

Consideration of all comments received within the comment period on discussion documents and exposure drafts, and to make modifications to proposed standards as considered appropriate in the light of the IPSASB's objectives

Publication of an IPSAS which includes a Basis for Conclusion that explains the steps in the IPSASB's due process and how the IPSASB reached is conclusions

Figure 3: The IPSASB's due process

The due process starts with a decision by the board whether a standard should be developed on a certain matter or not. If the IPSASB approves going further with a standard project, the IPSASB staff develop what is referred to as a project brief. Then, the board agrees on the project brief and sets a rough guideline for the further development of the standard. Depending on the project the IPSASB will either choose to develop an exposure draft directly or to start with a consultation paper and develop the exposure draft afterwards. Once the draft consultation paper has been completed by the IPSASB staff, the board issues its final remarks on the consultation paper and approves it. Usually, the consultation paper contains requests for comments on certain matters of the paper. The paper is made available to the general public on the website of the IFAC and can be commented on by interested parties. Following the phase of exposure for comment and subsequent revision by IPSASB employees, an exposure draft is presented to the board for approval. Once the IPSASB has approved the exposure draft, it is published and requests for comment are sought. Occasionally the IPSASB may reissue the exposure draft as such if there are any significant issues that remain to be solved. Based on the comments received the IPSASB will revise the proposed standard and finally approve it as a standard.

A majority of two thirds of the voting rights on the IPSASB is required for approval of consultation papers, exposure draft or standards. Each member of the IPSASB has one vote. The text of a pronouncement that is published by the IPSASB in English is deemed to be the approved version.

The general structure of an IPSAS is as follows:

▪ Contents
▪ Introduction
▪ Objective
▪ Scope
▪ Definitions
▪ Accounting policies
▪ Transitional provisions
▪ Effective date
▪ Appendices and/or Application Guidance
▪ Basis for Conclusion
▪ Comparison with the corresponding IFRS (where appropriate)

Table 5: Structure of an IPSAS

2.9 IPSASs for accrual basis of accounting and cash basis of accounting

Due to their financial sovereignty, jurisdictions such as nations or states have the authority to decide on how they want to structure public sector accounting within their jurisdiction. From an international perspective, only requirements relating to financial statistics have had an impact on public financial reporting to date. Public sector entities that keep their accounts in accordance with IPSASs can choose to use either accrual accounting or cash accounting. The IPSASB has decided to issue only one standard on the cash basis of accounting – the Cash Basis IPSAS. All other IPSASs are developed exclusively on the accrual basis of accounting – in line with the accounting concept applied in IFRSs. This documents the IPSASB's preference for this basis of accounting.

As a large number of the accrual basis IPSASs are based on IFRSs, the "Framework for the Presentation of Financial Statements" issued by the IASB is a key reference point in the application of the IPSASs. However, the IPSASB has realized that the specific nature of the public sector calls for an individual framework for the public sector. In cooperation with national standard setters, the IPSASB is taking the first steps towards drafting such a framework. The first results of the project were discussed at board meetings in 2009. The IPSASB issued the first in a series of consultation papers focused on the development of an international public sector conceptual framework on 30 September 2008.

2.10 Background to the introduction of international accounting standards for the public sector

Internationally, the (New) Public Management movement has gained outstanding importance in the public sector reform. One of the key components of this new way of managing public affairs is the reform of public sector accounting and financial reporting. This new financial governance model for public sector organizations often entails reforms of their budgets. The accrual basis of accounting constitutes a major reform element in this context.

A global trend of alignment of public sector accounting with the international accounting standards for the public sector is currently emerging. The table below gives an overview of major countries and regions that have decided to introduce IPSASs or similar accounting standards or have already done so.

Afghanistan*	Indonesia	Romania
Albania	Israel	Russia
Algeria	Latvia	Switzerland
Argentina	Lithuania	Slovakia
Brazil	Malaysia*	Spain
China	Morocco	South Africa

East and Southern Africa	Nepal	Ukraine
France	Netherlands	Uruguay
Ghana	Nigeria	Vietnam
Hungary	Norway	
India	Pakistan	

* Cash basis of accounting

Table 6: *Overview of selected countries that have decided to introduce IPSASs/similar accounting standards or have already done so (source: http://www. ipsasb.org, 1 July 2008)*

The IPSASB has also found that the public sector accounting practice in Australia, Canada, New Zealand, the UK and the United States is already largely in compliance with IPSASs. For example, Australia and UK use IFRSs as a basis for governmental accounting.

The supranational organizations listed below have also decided to introduce IPSASs. This is another fact underlining the growing importance of IPSASs.

- European Commission
- OECD
- NATO
- United Nations (including all its institutions, such as UNESCO, UNICEF, WFP, etc.)

Table 7: *Overview of supranational organizations that have decided to introduce IPSASs or have already done so (source: own research)*

The project launched by the United Nations and its institutions is one of the most significant and noteworthy cases worldwide of a transition to IPSASs.

In contrast to supranational organizations, which often adopt IPSASs directly, states have financial and legislative power and therefore tend to use this power to align their national accounting provisions to these standards instead of adopting them directly.

The adoption of international accounting standards ensures comparative and standardized information on finances and the economic situation of public sector entities across jurisdictions. Since IPSASs have been derived from IFRSs, they are able to build on an accounting basis that has been well established in the private sector over recent years. This common basis makes for convergence in private and public sector accounting for comparable matters – while at the same time allowing for divergence where rules specifically adapted to the public sector are required.

Because they are geared towards decision-making needs, the IPSASs provide the executive and legislature with a better basis for their decisions on the allocation of resources. The accrual basis IPSASs take account of operational performance indicators such as provisions or amortization and depreciation. This makes IPSASs a suitable basis for efficient and effective public management. The accrual basis IPSASs can thus promote action guided by the principle of intergenerational equity and make a contribution to sustainable administrative action.

The IPSASB has the aim of creating high-quality international accounting standards for the public sector such that they ensure a fair presentation of the financial position, financial performance and cash flows of public sector entities (cf. IPSAS 1.27). In addition, they are intended to achieve transparency in the presentation of the financial position of public sector entities (cf. paragraph 27 of the Preface to International Public Sector Accounting Standards). Finally, they serve to enhance the accountability of the executive and legislature. The objective of accounting in accordance with IPSASs is, on the one hand, to provide public decision-makers with relevant information and, on the other, to ensure accountability for the public funds and resources entrusted to the entity (cf. IPSAS 1.15).

The IPSASs can also make a significant contribution for national standard setters. They can be of help to the authorities responsible for public sector accounting (e.g., a specially established standard setter) or the legislature when amending or revising accrual basis standards.

2.11   Provisions for the transition from the cash basis to the accrual basis of accounting

The Cash Basis IPSAS recommends that public sector entities make voluntary disclosures on the accrual basis of accounting even if their financial statements are prepared using the cash basis of accounting. A public sector entity in transition from the cash basis to the accrual basis of accounting may want to include certain accrual basis disclosures in the financial statements during that phase. The status (e.g., audited or unaudited) and the part of the report that contains the additional disclosures (the notes to the financial statements or an extra section in the financial report) are determined by the nature of the disclosures (e.g., reliability and completeness) as well as the legislative environment and the legal provisions that apply to the financial statements within the jurisdiction.

The IPSASB has also set itself the aim of facilitating compliance with the accrual basis IPSASs by means of transitional provisions in certain standards. Once a public sector entity has decided to adopt accrual accounting in accordance with the IPSASs, the transitional provisions set forth the dates applicable for the transition. Upon expiry of the transitional provisions, the public sector entity is required to prepare its financial statements in compliance with accrual basis IPSASs in all respects. IPSAS 1 "Presentation of Financial Statements" includes the following requirements: "An entity whose financial statements comply with International Public Sector Accounting Standards should disclose that fact. Financial statements should not be described as complying with International Public Sector Accounting Standards unless they comply with all the requirements of each applicable International Public Sector Accounting Standard." (cf. paragraph 24 of the Preface to International Public Sector Accounting Standards). IPSAS 1 also requires disclosures on the extent to which the public sector entity has applied transitional provisions.

IPSASs containing transitional provisions grant public sector entities an additional period to achieve full compliance with certain accrual basis IPSASs or afford an exemption from certain duties for the first-time adoption of IPSASs. Subject to the approval of the competent national legislature or standard setter and the applicable statutory provisions, a public sector entity may choose to adopt accrual accounting in accordance with IPSASs. As of that point in time, the public sector entity is then required to comply with all accrual basis IPSASs. As mentioned earlier, however, it may also make use of the transitional provisions afforded by the individual IPSAS.

3   Measurement bases in accordance with IPSASs

The principal measurement bases for initial and for subsequent measurement in accordance with IPSASs include cost, fair value and present value. Since these measurement bases are fundamental to numerous IPSASs, they have been defined first.

In this context it has to be stated that the IPSASB covers measurement in phase 3 of its conceptual framework project (cf. chapter 2.6). Phase 3 will obviously have an impact on the measurement bases in accordance with IPSASs. Discussions of the board have shown that it will not be possible to specify a single measurement basis for all the elements of financial reporting. The IPSASB is in the process of discussing the appropriate measurement basis for the different types of assets and liabilities and the appropriate use of discount rates.

In addition to the principal measurement bases underlying the IPSASs, most of which correspond to those of IFRSs, certain IPSASs introduce further specific bases for initial or subsequent measurement such as **net realizable value** and **current replacement cost** in **IPSAS 12**, **recoverable (service) amount** in **IPSAS 17, 21** and **26** or **value in use** under **IPSAS 21** and **26**. These measurement bases are presented in more detail in the context of the relevant standard.

3.1   Cost

As defined in IPSAS 16.7 or 17.13, cost is the amount of cash or cash equivalents paid or the fair value of any other consideration given to acquire an asset at the time of its acquisition or construction. Cost thus also includes all consideration given in exchange for the asset subject to measurement, which is either the cash and cash equivalents paid for the acquisition or, for barter transactions for example, the fair value of the consideration at the date of acquisition.

As a rule, IPSASs use the generic term "cost" instead of distinguishing between acquisition and construction cost or costs of purchase and costs of conversion (cf. IPSAS 12, 16 and 17).

Acquisition cost/costs of purchase

Acquisition costs or costs of purchase are one of the key measurement bases (as under IFRS) for all assets acquired by a public sector entity (cf. IPSAS 12.18, 16.26 or 17.26). In accordance with IPSAS 17.26, for example, items of property, plant and equipment that qualify for recognition in the statement of financial position are recognized at cost. The individual elements of cost are listed in IPSAS 17.30 et seq.

Construction cost/costs of conversion

Construction costs or costs of conversion are the key measurement basis for all assets wholly or partly constructed by a public sector entity itself (cf. in particular IPSAS 12.20 and IPSAS 17.26). Such assets include self-constructed and internally used property, plant and equipment as well as work in progress and finished goods. In accordance with IPSAS 17.36, the cost of a self-constructed asset is determined using the same principles as for an acquired asset. If an entity produces similar assets for sale in the normal course of business or administrative operations, the cost of the asset is usually the same as the cost of constructing an asset for sale (cf. IPSAS 12, "Inventories"). Therefore, any internal surpluses are eliminated in arriving at such costs. Similarly, the cost of abnormal amounts of spoilage, labor, or other resources incurred in self-constructing an asset is not included in the cost of the asset.

Neither IPSASs nor IFRSs indicate that a distinction should be made between the production cost of property, plant and equipment and the costs of conversion of inventories. Commentaries on the IFRSs take this to mean that the production cost of property, plant and equipment incurred in making the asset available for use should be determined in the same way as the costs of conversion of inventories. The cost of self-constructed property, plant and equipment hence comprises full construction-related costs. For determining costs of conversion of inventories, please refer to IPSAS 12, "Inventories".

3.2   Fair value

Fair value is another of the principal measurement bases of IPSASs. It is referred to in measuring assets and liabilities for example in IPSAS 4, 9, 12, 13, 15, 16, 17, 21 and 26.

Fair value is defined as the amount for which an asset could be exchanged, or a liability settled, between knowledgeable, willing parties in an arm's length transaction. Fair value is also at the heart of the revaluation method for measuring property, plant and equipment after recognition as an asset.

It is of importance especially for the public sector that assets acquired in a non-exchange transaction are measured at fair value as at the date of acquisition (cf. IPSAS 17.27). Moreover, as a reference value for comparison with amortized cost, fair value plays an important role in impairment testing (cf. e.g., IPSAS 26.20 et seq.)

If the asset to be measured is publicly traded, e.g., on an exchange, determining fair value is comparatively straight-forward. If it is not publicly traded, IPSAS 26.40 requires fair value to be "based on the best information available", taking into account "the outcome of recent transactions for similar assets within the same industry" (also IPSAS 26.40).

3.3   Present value

The **present value of an asset** comprises the discounted cash flows expected to be generated by the asset in the ordinary course of operations. Accordingly, the **present value of a liability** comprises the discounted cash flows required to be paid to settle the liability in the ordinary course of operations.

For instance in exchange transactions for a consideration that have long-term payment terms, the present value of the monetary consideration serves as a basis to measure the outstanding receivable (cf. IPSAS 9.16). Another example are provisions, which are recognized at present value in accordance with IPSAS 19.53 if the effect of the time value of money relating to the settlement of the obligation is material.

II   Impact of the financial crisis on public sector accounting

1   Context and current developments

The year 2008 saw the deepest recession since the 1930s. An unprecedented series of government interventions in the financial sector has followed and the economy at large aims at restoring confidence in national financial institutions and supporting global demand. Governments have had to provide considerable financial resources to help the economy to recover from severe disruptions on the world's capital markets. The actions taken by governments involve significant expenditure of taxpayers' money.

The scale and breadth of this financial crisis and the complexity of the policy responses have created two crucial issues for public sector accounting. The first issue is simply to understand the nature of these unprecedented government interventions. While the developments are similar throughout all countries, no two countries' policy responses are identical. The second issue is to consider how these interventions should be reported in government accounts.

These interventions have taken place in many different ways. Public sector entities have granted guarantees, taken responsibility for toxic loans, performed fiscal support and made a number of purchases. Governments have put forward different sets of measures to counteract the economic downturn, with different emphasis on a particular policy according to the specific nature of the local environment, industry focus of the country, budget constraints, etc.

Interventions have typically included:

- Recapitalization and investments: Bank recapitalization has become fairly common in the current crisis, especially for financial institutions that are material to the financial system as a whole. In addition, some corporate entities have needed capital injections. As a result, public sector entities have become shareholders in banks and other corporate entities. In some cases corporate entities have even been nationalized (e.g., Freddie Mac and Fannie Mae in the US, Hypo Real Estate in Germany or Northern Rock in the UK).
- Takeover risks: Some direct asset purchases have been made in the wake of the crisis, with public sector entities purchasing illiquid or toxic bonds from banks. So-called "bad banks" have been set up around

the world as a means of allowing private banks to take problem assets off their books.

- Fiscal support: A wide range of measures have been taken, aimed at different target groups. In various countries around the world, economic stimulus packages offering direct subsidies have been set up to stimulate the economy as a whole. Many governments have also launched infrastructure investment programs (mainly transportation, housing, schools, universities, hospitals and energy). Supplementing these general programs, the targeted measures introduced range from liquidity support provided to individual market players in the form of credit lines and tax relief for certain enterprises and persons right through to support for household incomes (especially for persons with low income and the unemployed).
- Financial guarantees: In many countries, state guarantees have been provided for bank deposits, interbank loans and, in some cases, for bonds and even corporate loans.

Around the world, financial support has been provided mainly to enterprises in the banking, automotive, energy and real estate/construction industries. State aid was also directed towards small and medium-sized enterprises. In the US, government has taken several measures to provide support to the damaged US financial system. In 2008, a USD 700bn scheme was approved, known as the Troubled Asset Relief Programme (TARP). TARP allowed the United States Department of the Treasury to purchase or insure up to USD 700bn of "troubled" assets from US financial institutions. The American Recovery and Reinvestment Act of 2009 was signed into law on 17 February 2009. The measures are nominally worth a total of USD 787bn. The act includes federal tax relief, expansion of unemployment benefits and other social welfare provisions, and domestic spending on education, healthcare and infrastructure, including the energy sector. One of the main objectives of the act is to save three to four million jobs. In Canada, the "Economic Action Plan" will provide support in the region of CAD 30-40bn to the Canadian economy in 2009. The French government, for example, proposed a EUR 26bn plan, with EUR 11.6bn to support private companies and EUR 10.5bn for public investments. In Germany, parliament approved a EUR 32bn rescue package in November 2008. In 2009, a second rescue plan was approved including the spending of EUR 82bn over the next two years. In the UK one of the biggest challenges was the turmoil in the banking sector. The UK has spent GBP 94bn to prop up the Royal Bank of Scotland, HBOS and Lloyds TSB, as well as nationalizing Northern Rock and parts of Bradford & Bingley. The Treasury and the Bank of England have pledged hundreds of billions of pounds of further support for the fragile banking system. The Indian government has announced two stimulus packages, involving additional government expenditure of USD 8bn. The main focus of the Indian government has been to ensure adequate liquidity in the banking system.

In light of the strong governmental interventions, there is a need to reflect these actions appropriately in the financial reporting of public sector entities. National and international standard-setting bodies have developed guidance on how private sector entities should deal with the financial crisis, yet the debate on how to account for these interventions in the financial reporting of public sector entities has yet to be held. Many of the interventions are not directly addressed in currently existing public sector accounting standards because the underlying transactions are new for public sector entities. Especially during the global financial crisis, however, there is a need for a clear and fair presentation of the economic consequences of these interventions.

In May 2009, the IPSASB and the International Monetary Fund (IMF) formed a joint task force to exchange experiences about government interventions made in response to the global financial crisis and to consider how these interventions should be treated in financial statements. The aim of the task force is to achieve consistency in financial reporting between governments.

The public sector's response to the financial crisis as described above will have a significant impact on short and long-term budgets. This has given rise to political pressure in many jurisdictions, as citizens question the long-term financial consequences of the various interventions that have been adopted to deal with the crisis. The IPSASB has therefore set up a project on long-term fiscal sustainability and will publish a consultation paper entitled "Long-Term Fiscal Sustainability in the Context of General Purpose Financial Reporting" by October 2009.

2   Accounting issues relating to public sector interventions

The global financial crisis has raised a number of issues that have to be considered thoroughly in the analysis and development of accounting standards. In the light of the IPSASB's strategic aim to provide a complete set of accounting standards, a discussion has started on how the existing and future IPSASB's pronouncements may address relevant accounting issues relating to the different kinds of governmental interventions.

The recurrent use of the term "transparency" in the context of the discussion underlines that it represents one of the key values in financial reporting by governments. Transparency implies that general purpose financial reports must include all information necessary for accountability purposes. This leads to the question whether the current IPSASB's pronouncements give sufficient guidance on financial reporting of governmental interventions in order to achieve accountability.

Accounting for recapitalization or investments

As a result of the financial crisis, public sector entities have become shareholders in financial institutions and other corporate entities. In some cases, financial institutions and other corporate entities have even been nationalized. From the perspective of the public sector entity, consideration must now be given to how these interests should be accounted for and whether they need to be consolidated.

When a government purchases such assets directly, the question is how to measure these assets. When interests in financial institutions and other corporate entities are purchased, there is a risk that impairment losses may need to be recognized by the public sector entities in subsequent accounting periods. In general, these interventions – most of which relating to the acquisition of cash-generating assets – are addressed in IPSAS 26 "Impairment of Cash-Generating Assets". According to IPSAS 26.22 an entity must assess at each reporting date whether there is any indication that a cash-generating asset may be impaired. If any such indication exists, the entity estimates the recoverable amount of the asset. In order to determine whether a cash-generating asset is impaired, public sector entities must consider the indications listed in IPSAS 26.25. An impairment loss is recognized if the recoverable amount of an asset is less than its carrying amount (cf. IPSAS 26.72). However, the scope of that standard does not cover financial instruments. A new IPSAS ED 38 has been proposed, dealing with impairment and uncollectibility of financial assets (cf. ED 38.67 et seq.). Thus, in its entirety the IPSASB's pronouncements should comprise sufficient guidance regarding the treatment of impairment losses on purchases of assets as state intervention.

According to IPSAS 6, the acquired entities may be subject to consolidation in some cases. The decisive criterion for consolidation according to IPSAS 6.20 is control, which is the power to govern the financial and operating policies of another entity in order to benefit from its activities. Some might argue that consolidation is not required because control over the acquired entity is only temporary or because the activities of the acquired entity are dissimilar to those of the public sector entity. Under IPSAS 6, a controlled entity may be excluded from consolidation if there is evidence that (a) control is intended to be temporary because the controlled entity is acquired and held exclusively with a view to its disposal within 12 months from acquisition and (b) management is actively seeking a buyer (cf. IPSAS 6.21). However, a controlled entity is not excluded from consolidation under IPSASs when its activities are dissimilar to those of the other entities within the economic entity. In that case, relevant information is provided by disclosing additional information, for example by way of segment reporting (cf. IPSAS 6.27). In conclusion, IPSAS 6 implies that general purpose financial reports include all information necessary for accountability purposes.

During the financial crisis some governments acted through special purpose entities with no direct interest, often referred to as "bad banks". A bad bank is a financial institution created by a government to hold non-performing assets. Where government-sponsored rescue entities are formed as special purpose entities, there is the question of control that needs to be addressed.

Accounting for fiscal support

Against the backdrop of the financial crisis fiscal support has been implemented by means such as the purchase of goods and services for current use, the purchase of goods and services for the creation of future benefits (infrastructure investments or research spending), liquidity support, tax reduction or transfers (mainly for social security and social benefits).

Where fiscal support is provided by way of direct public expenditure, investments in infrastructure assets are a popular target of investments. Such infrastructure assets are mainly covered by IPSAS 17 (cf. IPSAS 17.21). Furthermore, the IPSASB is in the process of developing guidance for service concession arrangements, often referred to as public private partnerships (PPP, cf. IPSAS ED 43, "Service Concession Arrangements").

Where fiscal support takes the form of liquidity support involving credit lines rather than direct subsidies, the terms of the credit transactions need to be examined. Concessionary loans pose particular accounting issues to the public sector (cf. ED 38.AG83 to AG89). These are loans granted to or received by an entity at below market terms. They must be distinguished from the waiver of debt. A waiver of debt results from loans initially granted or received at market terms where the intention of either party to the loan has changed subsequent to its initial issue or receipt. This distinction determines whether below market conditions are considered in the initial recognition or measurement of the loan, or as part of the subsequent measurement or derecognition. Where the concessionary loan is granted by a public sector entity, any difference between the fair value of the loan and the transaction price is recognized as an expense in surplus or deficit at initial recognition (cf. ED 38.AG88 (b)).

To sum up one may conclude that IPSASs give sufficient guidance to achieve accountability on the issues relating to fiscal support. However, that does not hold true for future tax reduction programs which have been announced by several governments. These programs will lead to future financial burdens because they will impair the power to tax. As the power to tax is not recognized as an intangible asset (cf. ED 40.4f; see discussion on framework project in chapter 2.6), there is no point to account for announced tax reduction programs.

Accounting for financial guarantees

As a consequence of the financial crisis, many public sector entities have provided financial guarantees to banks and corporate entities. As long as the outflow of resources embodying economic benefits or service potential is not probable, financial guarantees fall into the category of contingent liabilities (cf. IPSAS 19.18, 19.20 and 19.37), which, in accordance with IPSAS 19.35, may however not be recognized in the statement of financial position. Accordingly, financial guarantees are treated as an off-balance sheet transaction (cf. IPSAS 19.36 and 19.100), in contrast to direct liquidity support which is reported in the statement of financial position.

In the public sector, financial guarantees are frequently provided for no consideration or for nominal consideration to further the entity's economic and social objectives. In the current financial crisis, financial guarantees have been used to restore confidence in, and protect the stability of, the financial markets. From an accounting point of view there is the difficulty of identifying an accurate measurement. In cases of contractual financial guarantees for nominal consideration, the transaction price related to a financial guarantee contract does not reflect fair value because recognition on the basis of the transaction price would not accurately reflect the issuer's exposure to financial risk.

ED 38 now provides guidance on the accounting treatment of contractual financial guarantees. The IPSASB has concluded that financial guarantee contracts issued for no consideration or for nominal consideration (non-exchange transaction) should be accounted for as financial instruments (cf.

ED 38.AG3). At initial recognition, where no fee is charged or where the consideration is not fair value, a public sector entity firstly considers whether the fair value can be obtained through observation of quoted prices available in an active market for financial guarantee contracts directly equivalent to that entered into (level one). Where there is no active market for a directly equivalent guarantee contract, public sector entities should apply a mathematical valuation technique to obtain a fair value (level two). Alternatively, the principles of IPSAS 19 for initial recognition are applied (level three).

In summary it can be concluded that the application of IPSASs on financial guarantee contracts is sufficient from an accountability point of view. However, it has to be stated that currently IPSASs contain no specific guidance dealing with non-contractual financial guarantees announced by governments. For example, a government may give general deposit guarantees to its citizens. This gives rise to financial risks which are not shown in the general purpose financial reports. Finally, one has to add that as soon as the outflow of resources becomes probable, non-contractual guarantees announced by governments may give rise to a provision in accordance with IPSAS 19.18 ff.

III   Overview of accrual basis IPSASs

IPSAS 1: Presentation of Financial Statements

Objective

IPSAS 1 provides the bases of presentation for **general purpose financial statements** in order to ensure comparability on the one hand with the entity's financial statements of previous periods and, on the other, with the financial statements of other public sector entities. The standard sets out overall requirements of the presentation of financial statements prepared under the **accrual basis of accounting**, and provides guidance for the structure and minimum requirements of the content of such financial statements. The recognition and measurement of specific transactions and other events, and the corresponding disclosure requirements are dealt with in other International Public Sector Accounting Standards.

The IFRS on which the IPSAS is based

IAS 1 "Presentation of Financial Statements"

Content

Principal definitions

Assets are resources controlled by an entity as a result of past events and from which future economic benefits or service potential are expected to flow to the entity.

Liabilities are present obligations of the entity arising from past events, the settlement of which is expected to result in an outflow from the entity of resources embodying economic benefits or service potential.

Net assets/equity is the residual interest in the assets of the entity after deducting all its liabilities.

Revenue is the gross inflow of economic benefits or service potential during the reporting period when those inflows result in an increase in net assets/equity, other than increases relating to contributions from owners.

Expenses are decreases in economic benefits or service potential during the reporting period in the form of outflows or consumption of assets or incurrences of liabilities that result in decreases in net assets/equity, other than those relating to distributions to owners.

The term **economic entity** means a group of entities comprising a controlling entity and one or more controlled entities.

Scope

IPSAS 1 is of particular significance for the financial reporting of public sector entities. It is applicable for all general purpose financial statements prepared under the accrual basis of accounting.

Purpose of financial statements

The objective of **general purpose financial statements** is to provide information to meet the needs of those users of financial statements who are not in a position to demand reporting adapted to their needs. The users of general purpose financial statements include taxpayers, members of parliaments, creditors, suppliers, the media and public sector employees.

Financial statements prepared in accordance with IPSASs must present fairly the financial position, financial performance and cash flows of an entity (cf. IPSAS 1.27). To meet this requirement, a public sector entity must first of all observe general qualitative characteristics of financial reporting.

Such "qualitative characteristics of financial reporting" are fundamental principles for preparing financial statements in accordance with IPSASs. Despite the fact that they are presented only as an appendix to IPSAS 1, they are an integral part of that IPSAS. The four principal qualitative characteristics are understandability, relevance, reliability and comparability. These principles ensure that the users of financial statements are provided with useful information for decision-making purposes.

Furthermore, IPSAS 1 defines general standards for the preparation of financial statements. These include the going concern assumption (IPSAS 1.38 et seq.), consistency of presentation (IPSAS 1.42 et seq.), materiality and aggregation (IPSAS 1.45 et seq.), offsetting (IPSAS 1.48 et seq.) and comparative information (IPSAS 1.53 et seq.).

Components of financial statements

A complete set of financial statements in accordance with accrual basis IPSASs comprises the following components listed in IPSAS 1.21:

- A statement of financial position
- A statement of financial performance
- A statement of changes in net assets/equity
- A cash flow statement

- When the entity makes publicly available its approved budget, a comparison of budget and actual amounts either as separate additional financial statements or as a budget column in the financial statements
- Notes, comprising a summary of significant accounting policies and other explanatory notes

Public sector entities whose financial statements comply with IPSASs should disclose that fact in the notes to the financial statements. Financial statements that do not comply with all the requirements of the applicable IPSASs must not be described as complying with IPSASs. Only in extremely rare circumstances when the management of a public sector entity has reached the conclusion that compliance with a requirement in an IPSAS would give a misleading presentation may an entity depart from this requirement.

When preparing financial statements, a public sector entity is required to assess whether it can be assumed that it is able to continue as a going concern (cf. IPSAS 1.38). Generally, financial statements of a public sector entity are prepared on a going concern basis unless there is an intention to liquidate the entity or discontinue business or administrative operations, or there is no alternative but to do so. Should the management of a public sector entity have significant doubt as to the entity's ability to continue as a going concern, such uncertainties must be disclosed. Where financial statements are not prepared on a going concern basis, the public sector entity is required to disclose the fact, together with the reasons for that assessment as well as the basis on which the financial statements are prepared (cf. IPSAS 1.38).

The presentation and classification of items in the financial statements must be consistent from one period to another unless required otherwise by a significant change in the nature of the entity's operations or a change in one or more IPSASs (cf. IPSAS 1.42).

Each material class of items in the financial statements must be presented separately (cf. IPSAS 1.45). Aggregating items of a different nature of function is permitted only if they are immaterial individually.

Assets and liabilities, and revenue and expenses, may not be offset unless offsetting is expressly permitted or required by another IPSAS (cf. IPSAS 1.48).

Comparative prior-period information must be presented for all amounts shown in the financial statements and notes (cf. IPSAS 1.53). Comparative information is included for narrative and descriptive information where relevant to an understanding of the current period's financial statements. If the presentation or classification is amended, comparative amounts are also

35

reclassified unless it is impracticable to do so. The nature and amount reclassified and reason for the reclassification must be disclosed.

Financial statements are presented at least annually (cf. IPSAS 1.66). If the reporting date changes and financial statements are presented for a period other than one year, disclosure thereof is required.

Statement of financial position

IPSAS 1 specifies minimum line items to be presented in the statement of financial position and the statement of financial performance, and includes guidance for identifying whether additional line items, headings and sub-totals are required (see table 7).

There is no particular requirement as to the format of presentation of the statement of financial position (cf. IPSAS 1.90). It may be presented either in account form or vertical form.

In accordance with IPSAS 1.70, the statement of financial position presents assets and liabilities classified by maturity as current and non-current. An exception may only be made if classification by liquidity provides more reliable and relevant information.

Assets and liabilities are classified as current when they are expected to be recovered or settled in the course of ordinary operations or within 12 months of the reporting date (for further details, cf. IPSAS 1.76 et seq. and IPSAS 1.80 et seq.). A public sector entity must disclose the amount expected to be recovered or settled after more than 12 months for each asset and liability line item that combines amounts expected to be recovered or settled both within 12 months of the reporting date or thereafter.

Information to be presented on the face of the statement of financial position:
a)   Property, plant and equipment
b)   Investment property
c)   Intangible assets
d)   Financial assets (excluding amounts shown under (e), (g), (h) and (i))
e)   Investments accounted for using the equity method
f)   Inventories
g)   Recoverables from non-exchange transactions (taxes and transfers)
h)   Receivables from exchange transactions
i)   Cash and cash equivalents
j)   Taxes and transfers payable
k)   Payables under exchange transactions
l)   Provisions
m)   Financial liabilities (excluding amounts shown under (j), (k) and (l))
n)   Minority interests, presented within net assets/equity
o)   Net asset/equity attributable to owners of the controlling entity

Table 8:   Minimum requirements of the statement of financial position in accordance with IPSAS 1.88

The specific recognition and measurement requirements for the individual line items of the statement of financial position are set forth in the relevant standards instead of in IPSAS 1.

Statement of financial performance

The minimum classification of a statement of financial performance is set forth in IPSAS 1.102 (see table 8).

Public sector entities are required to present an analysis of expenses either in the statement of financial performance or in the notes (cf. IPSAS 1.109 et seq.). The expenses are classified either by nature or by their function within the entity, depending on which classification provides more reliable and relevant information.

If an entity decides to classify expenses by function, it must also provide a presentation by nature of expense in the notes, including depreciation and amortization expense and employee benefits expense.

Information to be presented on the face of the statement of financial performance:

		20X8	20X7
a)	Revenue	X	X
b)	Finance costs	X	X
c)	Share of the surplus or deficit of associates and joint ventures accounted for using the equity method	X	X
d)	Pre-tax gain or loss recognized on the disposal of assets or settlement of liabilities attributable to discontinuing operations	X	X
e)	Surplus or deficit	X	X

Table 9:   Minimum requirements of the statement of financial performance in accordance with IPSAS 1.102

Statement of changes in net assets/equity

IPSAS 1 also contains provisions regarding the presentation of a statement of changes in net assets/equity. The aim is to provide a break-down of movements in equity, which are not recognized in surplus or deficit nor, accordingly, in the statement of financial performance (cf. IPSAS 1.118 et seq.).

Information to be presented on the face of the statement of changes in net assets/equity:

a) Surplus or deficit for the period
b) Each item of revenue and expense for the period that, as required by other standards, is recognized directly in net assets/equity, and the total of these items
c) Total revenue and expense for the period (calculated as the sum of (a) and (b)), showing separately the total amounts attributable to owners of the controlling entity and to minority interest
d) For each component of net assets/equity separately disclosed, the effects of changes in accounting policies and corrections of errors recognized in accordance with IPSAS 3

Table 10: Minimum requirements of the statement of changes in net assets/equity in accordance with IPSAS 1.118

By analogy to IAS 1.97, public sector entities are required to present the amounts of transactions with owners acting in their capacity as owners either in the statement of changes in net assets/equity or in the notes, and to show distributions or allocations to owners separately.

Cash flow statement

The requirements of a cash flow statement and its structure are governed by IPSAS 2.

Notes to the financial statements

IPSAS 1 contains extensive minimum disclosure requirements for the notes to the financial statements. IPSAS 1 prescribes the following disclosures in the notes, supplementing the disclosures required by individual IPSASs:

- Disclosure of the measurement bases used
- Disclosure of accounting policies used that are relevant to an understanding of the financial statements
- Information required by IPSASs that is not presented on the face of the statement of financial position, statement of financial performance, statement of changes in equity or cash flow statements
- Disclosure of the extent to which transitional provisions have been used
- Presentation of the judgments that management has made in the process of applying the public sector entity's accounting policies that have the

most significant effect on the amounts recognized in the financial statements

- Disclosure of the key assumptions concerning the future, and other key sources of estimation uncertainty, that have a significant risk of causing a material adjustment to the carrying amounts of assets and liabilities within the next financial year. In respect of those assets and liabilities the notes should include details of their nature and their carrying amount as at the reporting date.
- Disclosure of the domicile and legal form of the entity
- A description of the nature of the entity's operations
- A reference to the relevant legislation governing the entity's operations
- Disclosure of the name of the controlling entity and the ultimate controlling entity of the economic entity

The implementation guidance to IPSAS 1 provides illustrative financial statements comprising illustrative statements of financial position, statements of financial performance and statements of changes in net assets/equity for public sector entities.

Effective date

Periods beginning on or after 1 January 2008.

IPSAS 2: Cash Flow Statement

Objective

This standard requires the presentation of information about the historical changes in cash and cash equivalents of an entity by means of a cash flow statement which classifies cash flows during the period by operating, investing and financing activities. The cash flow statement identifies the sources of cash inflows, the items on which cash was expended during the reporting period, and the cash and cash equivalents as at the reporting date. The cash flow statement is intended to provide users of financial statements with information for both accountability and decision-making purposes. Cash flow information allows users to understand how a public sector entity raised the cash it required to fund its business and administrative operations and how that cash was used.

The IFRS on which the IPSAS is based

IAS 7 "Cash Flow Statements"

Content

Principal definitions

The **cash flow statement** reports the cash flows during a reporting period and serves to analyze the changes in cash and cash equivalents.

Cash flows are inflows and outflows of cash and cash equivalents.

Cash comprises cash on hand and demand deposits, whereas **cash equivalents** are short-term, highly liquid investments that are readily convertible to known amounts of cash and which are subject to an insignificant risk of changes in value. In some countries, short-term bank borrowings (overdraft facilities) are also considered to be cash provided they are payable on demand, thereby forming an integral part of the entity's cash management (cf. IPSAS 2.10). Cash generally does not include equity investments.

41

Presentation, structure and content of the cash flow statement

The cash flows are reported separately by operating activities, investing activities and financing activities.

Cash flows from operating activities of a public sector entity are an indicator of the extent to which a public sector entity is financed by taxes or the sale of goods and services. Examples of cash flows from operating activities in accordance with IPSAS 2.22 are:

a)	Cash receipts from taxes, levies and fines
b)	Cash receipts from charges for goods and services provided by the entity
c)	Cash receipts from grants or transfers and other appropriations or other budget authority made by central government or other public sector entities
d)	Cash receipts from royalties, fees, commissions and other revenue
e)	Cash payments to other public sector entities to finance their operations (not including loans)
f)	Cash payments to suppliers for goods and services
g)	Cash payments to and on behalf of employees
h)	Cash receipts and payments of an insurance entity for premiums and claims, annuities and other policy benefits
i)	Cash payments of local property taxes or income taxes (where appropriate) in relation to operating activities
j)	Cash receipts or payments from contracts held for dealing or trading purposes
k)	Cash receipts or payments from discontinued operations
l)	Cash receipts or payments in relation to litigation settlements

Table 11: Examples of cash flow from operating activities

In accordance with IPSAS 2.27 cash flows for operating activities are reported using either the **direct** method recommended by the IPSASB or the **indirect method**. Public sector entities reporting cash flows using the direct method are encouraged to provide a reconciliation of the surplus/deficit from ordinary activities (statement of financial performance) with the net cash flow from operating activities (cash flow statement) either in the cash flow statement or the notes.

Cash flows from investing activities mainly consist of cash payments to acquire resources that are intended to contribute to the entity's future public service delivery. Examples of cash flows from investing activities in accordance with IPSAS 2.25 are:

a)	Cash payments to acquire property, plant and equipment, intangibles and other long-term assets. These payments include those relating to capitalized development costs and self-constructed property, plant and equipment.
b)	Cash receipts from sales of property, plant and equipment, intangibles and other long-term assets
c)	Cash payments to acquire equity or debt instruments of other entities and interests in joint ventures (other than payments for those instruments considered to be cash equivalents or those held for dealing or trading purposes)
d)	Cash receipts from sales of equity or debt instruments of other entities and interests in joint ventures (other than receipts for those instruments considered to be cash equivalents and those held for dealing or trading purposes)
e)	Cash advances and loans made to other parties (other than advances and loans made by a public financial institution)
f)	Cash receipts from the repayment of advances and loans made to other parties (other than advances and loans of a public financial institution)
g)	Cash payments for futures contracts, forward contracts, option contracts and swap contracts except when the contracts are held for dealing or trading purposes, or the payments are classified as financing activities
h)	Cash receipts from futures contracts, forward contracts, option contracts and swap contracts except when the contracts are held for dealing or trading purposes, or the receipts are classified as financing activities

Table 12:   Examples of cash flows from investing activities

Cash flows from financing activities present valuable information in that they show future claims by providers of capital to the entity. Examples of cash flows from financing activities in accordance with IPSAS 2.26 are:

a)	Cash proceeds from issuing debentures, loans, notes, bonds, mortgages and other short or long-term borrowings
b)	Cash repayments of amounts borrowed
c)	Cash payments by a lessee for the reduction of the outstanding liability relating to a finance lease

Table 13:   Examples of cash flows from financing activities

Public sector entities are required to report separately all major classes of gross cash receipts and gross cash payments arising from investing and financing activities unless the standard expressly permits reporting cash flows on a net basis (cf. IPSAS 2.32-35).

Cash flows arising from transactions in a foreign currency are recorded in an entity's functional currency by applying to the foreign currency amount the exchange rate between the functional currency and the foreign currency at the date of the cash flow. For the functional currency concept, see IPSAS 4.

Cash flows from interest and dividends received and paid are each disclosed separately and classified in a consistent manner from period to period as either operating, investing or financing activities.

Cash flows arising from taxes on net surplus are classified as cash flows from operating activities unless they can be allocated to specific financing or investing activities.

The aggregate cash flows arising from acquisitions and from disposals of subsidiaries or other business units are presented separately and classified as investing activities. Further specific disclosures are required.

In accordance with IPSAS 2.56, entities are required to disclose the components of cash and cash equivalents and to present a reconciliation of the amounts in their cash flow statement with the equivalent items reported in the statement of financial position.

The following table is an example of the structure using the direct method:

	20X8	20X9
Cash flows from operating activities		
Receipts		
Taxation	X	X
Sales of goods and services	X	X
Grants	X	X
Interest received	X	X
Other receipts	X	X
Payments		
Employee costs	(X)	(X)
Superannuation	(X)	(X)
Suppliers	(X)	(X)
Interest paid	(X)	(X)
Other payments	(X)	(X)
Net cash flows from operating activities	X	X
Cash flows from investing activities		
Purchase of property, plant and equipment	(X)	(X)
Proceeds from the sale of property, plant and equipment	X	X
Proceeds from the sale of investments	X	X
Purchase of foreign currency securities	(X)	(X)
Net cash flows from investing activities	(X)	(X)
Cash flows from financing activities		
Proceeds from borrowings	X	X
Repayment of borrowings	(X)	(X)
Distribution/dividend to government	(X)	(X)
Net cash flows from financing activities	X	X
Net increase/(decrease) in cash and cash equivalents	X	X
Cash and cash equivalents at the beginning of the reporting period	X	X
Cash and cash equivalents at the end of the reporting period	X	X

Table 14: Example of a cash flow statement prepared using the direct method in accordance with IPSAS 2 (cf. Appendix to IPSAS 2)

Effective date

Periods beginning on or after 1 July 2001.

IPSAS 3: Accounting Policies, Changes in Accounting Estimates and Errors

Objective

This standard governs the process of selecting and changing accounting policies, as well as the accounting treatment and disclosure of changes in accounting policies, changes in accounting estimates and the corrections of errors. IPSAS 3 sets out a hierarchy of authoritative guidance for management to consider in the absence of a standard that specifically applies to an item. The standard is intended to enhance the relevance and reliability of a public sector entity's financial statements as well as comparability of those financial statements over time and with the financial statements of other entities.

Disclosure requirements for accounting policies, except those for changes in accounting policies, are set out in IPSAS 1, "Presentation of Financial Statements".

The IFRS on which the IPSAS is based

IAS 8 "Accounting Policies, Changes in Accounting Estimates and Errors"

Content

Principal definitions

Accounting policies are the specific principles, bases, conventions, rules and practices applied by an entity in preparing and presenting financial statements.

Retrospective application is applying a new accounting policy to transactions, other events and conditions as if that policy had always been applied.

Prospective application of a change in accounting policy and of recognizing the effect of a change in an accounting estimate, respectively, are

    (a) Applying the new accounting policy to transactions, other events and conditions occurring after the date as at which the policy is changed

    (b) Recognizing the effect of the change in the accounting estimate in the current and future periods affected by the change

A **change in accounting estimate** is an adjustment of the carrying amount of an asset or a liability, or the amount of the periodic consumption of an asset, that results from the assessment of the present status of, and expected future

47

benefits and obligations associated with, assets and liabilities. Changes in accounting estimates result from new information or new developments and, accordingly, are not correction of errors.

Omissions or misstatements of items are **material** if they could, individually or collectively, influence the decisions or assessments of users made on the basis of the financial statements.

Prior period errors are omissions from, and misstatements in, the entity's financial statements for one or more prior periods arising from a failure to use, or misuse of, (a) reliable information that was available when financial statements for those periods were authorized for issue and (b) could reasonably be expected to have been obtained and taken into account in the preparation and presentation of those financial statements.

General provisions

When an IPSAS expressly refers to a transaction, other event or condition, the accounting policies applicable to that item are determined by applying the standard and considering any relevant Implementation Guidance issued by the IPSASB for the standard.

In the absence of an IPSAS applicable to a transaction, other event or condition, management must use judgment in developing and applying an accounting policy to achieve disclosures that are:

- Relevant to the decision-making needs of users, and
- Reliable, in that the financial statements:
    - Represent faithfully the financial position, financial performance and cash flows of the entity
    - Reflect the economic substance of transactions, other events and conditions and not merely the legal form
    - Are neutral, i.e., free from bias
    - Are prudent
    - Are complete in all material aspects

In the absence of an IPSAS applicable to a transaction, other event or condition, IPSAS 3 refers to the **hierarchy of authoritative guidance** and prescribes that management determine the relevant accounting policies by referring to the following sources in the order given below:

- First, the requirements and guidance in IPSASs dealing with similar and related issues are to be consulted.

- Second, management should refer to the definitions, recognition and measurement criteria for assets, liabilities, revenue and expenses described in other IPSASs.
- Finally, management may also consult recent pronouncements issued by other standard setters and renowned public or private sector practitioners, provided they do not conflict with the above sources. These include in particular the pronouncements issued by the International Accounting Standards Board (IASB) (including the Framework), International Financial Reporting Standards (IFRSs) and International Accounting Standards (IASs) and all interpretations published by the International Financial Reporting Interpretations Committee (IFRIC) or its predecessor, the Standing Interpretations Committee (SIC).

Changes in accounting policies

Changes in accounting policy may be made only when required by an IPSAS or when such changes result in the financial statements providing reliable and more relevant information about the effects of transactions, other events or conditions on the entity's financial position, financial performance or cash flows.

A change from one basis of accounting to another, e.g., from cash basis to accrual basis of accounting, or changes in the accounting treatment, recognition or measurement within the same basis of accounting (e.g., accrual basis of accounting) are deemed changes in a public sector entity's accounting in accordance with IPSAS 3.19 and 3.20.

By contrast, (a) the application of an accounting policy for transactions, other events or conditions that differ in substance from those previously occurring and (b) the application of a new accounting policy for transactions, other events or conditions that did not occur previously or that were immaterial are **not** changes in accounting policies.

When applying changes in accounting policies resulting from the initial application of a standard, public sector entities must consider any specific transitional provisions (cf. IPSAS 3.24 (a)).

When changing an accounting policy upon initial adoption of a standard that does not include any specific transitional provisions applying to that change, entities must apply the change retrospectively. The same applies when entities change an accounting policy on a **voluntary** basis (cf. IPSAS 3.24(b)).

When retrospective application in accordance with IPSAS 3.24 (a) or (b) is required, a change in accounting policy must be applied retrospectively unless it is impracticable to determine either the period-specific effects or the cumulative effect of the change.

When a change in accounting policy is applied retrospectively, public sector entities adjust the opening balance of each affected component of net assets/equity for the earliest prior period presented and the other comparative amounts disclosed for each prior period presented as if the new accounting policy had always been applied.

Consistency principle

Accounting policies must be applied **consistently** for similar transactions unless a standard permits or requires categorization of items for which different policies may be appropriate. If a standard requires or permits such categorization, an appropriate accounting policy is selected and applied consistently to each category.

Changes in accounting estimates

The effects of **changes in accounting estimates** are recognized prospectively in accordance with IPSAS 3.41 through surplus or deficit

    (a)   in the period of change if the change affects the period only (e.g., changes in the estimate of a doubtful receivable), or

    (b)   in the period of the change and future periods if the change affects both the reporting period and future periods (e.g., changes in accounting estimates relating to the useful life of an asset subject to depreciation).

To the extent that a change in an accounting estimate gives rise to changes in assets and liabilities or relates to an item of net assets/equity, it is recognized by adjusting the carrying amount of the related asset, liability or net assets/equity item in the period of change (cf. IPSAS 3.42).

Corrections of errors

Public sector entities are required to correct any **material prior period errors** retrospectively in the first complete set of financial statements authorized for issue after their discovery by: (a) restating the comparative amounts for the prior periods presented in which the error occurred; or (b) if the error occurred before the earliest prior period presented, restating the opening balances of assets, liabilities and net assets/equity for the earliest prior period presented.

An exception to this rule may be made when it is impracticable to determine either the period-specific effects or the cumulative effect of the error.

Effective date

Periods beginning on or after 1 January 2008.

IPSAS 4: The Effects of Changes in Foreign Exchange Rates

Objective

There are two ways for public sector entities to enter into business relations at an international level. Such business relations can either take the form of foreign currency transactions with a foreign business partner or business or administrative operations performed abroad. In addition, public sector entities may present their financial statements in a foreign currency. The objective of this standard is to prescribe how public sector entities should account for foreign currency transactions and foreign operations in their financial statements and how to translate financial statements into a presentation currency. In particular it addresses general issues such as the exchange rates to be used and how the financial effects of changes in exchange rates should be accounted for in the financial statements.

The IFRS on which the IPSAS is based

IAS 21 "The Effects of Changes in Foreign Exchange Rates"

Content

Principal definitions

Functional currency is the currency of the primary economic environment in which the entity operates. The primary economic environment of an entity is normally the one in which it primarily generates and expends cash.

Presentation currency is the currency in which the financial statements are presented.

Scope

Public sector entities preparing financial statements under the accrual basis of accounting are required to apply IPSAS 4:

    (a) In accounting for transactions and balances in foreign currencies, except for those derivative transactions and balances that are within the scope of the relevant international or national accounting standards dealing with the recognition and measurement of financial instruments

(b) In translating the financial performance and financial position of foreign operations that are included in the financial statements of the entity by consolidation, proportionate consolidation or by the equity method

(c) In translating an entity's financial performance and financial position into a presentation currency

Functional currency concept

The factors relevant for determining a public sector entity's functional currency are listed in IPSAS 4.11 et seq.

The functional currency reflects the underlying transactions, events and conditions that are of relevance to the public sector entity. Once it has been determined, a functional currency may therefore be changed only if there has been a change in the underlying transactions, events and conditions.

If the functional currency is the currency of a hyperinflationary economy, the requirements of IPSAS 10 "Financial Reporting in Hyperinflationary Economies" must be observed in the entity's financial statements.

Accounting for transactions in foreign currencies

As public sector entities tend to have only very few transactions in foreign currency and conduct business or administrative operations abroad on a small scale only, IPSAS 4 is not as relevant for the public sector as the corresponding IFRS is for the private sector.

In preparing financial statements, every public sector entity – whether a stand-alone entity, an entity with foreign operations (e.g., a parent) or a foreign operation (e.g., a subsidiary or a branch) – decides on its **functional currency**.

Upon **initial recognition, foreign currency transactions** are recognized in the **functional currency** by translating the foreign currency amount at the **spot exchange rate** between the functional currency and foreign currency on the date of the transaction.

Reporting in subsequent periods (cf. IPSAS 4.27): At each reporting date

(a) Foreign currency **monetary items** are translated using the **closing rate**.

(b) Non-monetary items that are measured in terms of historical cost in a foreign currency are translated using the exchange rate at the date of the transaction.

(c) **Non-monetary items** that are measured at **fair value** in a foreign currency are translated using the exchange rates at the date when the fair value was determined.

Exchange differences arising on the settlement of monetary items and on translating monetary items at rates different from those used upon initial recognition are recognized in surplus or deficit. Exchange differences arising from a monetary item that forms part of the reporting entity's net investment in a foreign (business or administrative) operation are recognized as a separate component of net assets/equity in the consolidated financial statements. Consolidated financial statements also include the separate financial statements of foreign operations. Upon disposal of the net investment the associated exchange differences are recognized in surplus or deficit.

Translating to the presentation currency

IPSAS 4 permits reporting entities in the public sector to choose their presentation currency (or currencies) freely. In addition, the financial position and financial performance of every individual entity within the reporting entity whose functional currency differs from the presentation currency must be translated to the reporting entity's presentation currency. The translation of financial statements to the presentation currency is governed by IPSAS 4.42 et seq. When translating a foreign (business or administrative) operation, the requirements of IPSAS 4.49 et seq. must also be observed.

The financial performance and financial position of a public sector entity whose functional currency is not the currency of a hyperinflationary economy are translated into a different presentation currency as follows:

- Assets and liabilities for each statement of financial position presented (i.e., including comparatives) are translated at the closing rate at the date of that statement of financial position.
- Revenue and expenses in all statements of financial performance (i.e., including comparative information) are translated at exchange rates at the date of the transaction and all resulting exchange differences are recognized as a separate component of net assets/equity.
- Special rules apply for translating the financial performance and financial position of an entity whose functional currency is the currency of a hyperinflationary economy into a presentation currency (cf. IPSAS 4.48).

Changing the functional currency

When **changing the functional currency** public sector entities must apply the translation procedures applicable to the new functional currency **prospectively** as of the date of transition.

Effective date

Periods beginning on or after 1 January 2010.

IPSAS 5: Borrowing Costs

Objective

IPSAS 5 governs the accounting treatment for borrowing costs. In general, it requires borrowing costs to be expensed immediately, but does permit, as an allowed alternative treatment, the capitalization of borrowing costs that are directly attributable to the acquisition, construction or production of a qualifying asset.

The IFRS on which the IPSAS is based

IAS 23 "Borrowing Costs"

Content

Principal definitions

Borrowing costs are interest and other expenses incurred by an entity in connection with the borrowing of funds. Borrowing costs include interest on overdraft facilities or short-term and long-term borrowings, the amortization of discounts or premiums on borrowings, amortization of ancillary costs incurred in connection with the arrangement of borrowings, finance charges for finance leases and exchange differences arising from foreign currency borrowings to the extent that they qualify as an adjustment to interest costs.

A **qualifying asset** is an asset that necessarily takes a substantial period of time to get ready for its intended use or sale. Examples relevant for the public sector include office buildings, hospitals, and infrastructure assets such as roads, bridges and power generation facilities. Moreover, inventories that require a substantial period of time to get ready for their intended use or sale are also qualifying assets (IPSAS 5.13).

Recognition

Public sector entities can refer to the debt market to finance qualifying assets.

IPSAS 5 generally provides for two alternative methods with respect to the accounting treatment for borrowing costs:

- Under the **benchmark treatment**, borrowing costs are recognized as an expense in the period in which they are incurred. In this case, the borrowings do not need to be allocated directly to the individual assets. The benchmark treatment is the preferred method pursuant to IPSAS 5 (see the section "Comments on IPSAS 5" below).

56

- Under the **allowed alternative treatment**, borrowing costs that are directly attributable to the acquisition, construction or production of a qualifying asset are capitalized as part of the cost of that asset.

When a public sector entity decides to adopt the allowed alternative treatment, IPSAS 5.20 requires the treatment to be applied consistently to all borrowing costs that are directly attributable to the acquisition, construction or production of the qualifying assets of that public sector entity.

If funds are borrowed specifically for the purpose of obtaining a qualifying asset, the amount of borrowing costs eligible for capitalization on that asset is determined by deducting any investment income on the temporary investment of those borrowings from the actual borrowing costs incurred during the period.

For funds that are initially borrowed without a specific purpose in mind and then at a later stage used for the purpose of obtaining a qualifying asset, the amount of borrowing costs eligible for capitalization is determined by applying a capitalization rate to the expenditures on that asset. The capitalization rate is the weighted average of the borrowing costs applicable to the borrowings of the entity that are outstanding during the period, other than borrowings made specifically for the purpose of obtaining a qualifying asset. The amount of borrowing costs capitalized during a period may not exceed the total borrowing costs incurred during that period.

Capitalization of the borrowing costs as part of the cost of a qualifying asset commences when either (a) expenditure is incurred on the asset, (b) borrowing costs are incurred, or (c) the work necessary to get the asset ready for its intended use or sale has started.

Capitalization of borrowing costs is **suspended** when active development of the qualifying asset is interrupted during an extended period of time.

Capitalization of borrowing costs ceases when substantially all the activities necessary to prepare the qualifying asset for its intended use or sale are complete.

When the **construction of a qualifying asset is completed in parts** and each part is capable of being used while construction continues on other parts, capitalization of borrowing costs ceases provided that substantially all the activities necessary to prepare that part for its intended use or sale are completed. An office complex comprising several buildings, each of which can be used individually, is an example of a qualifying asset for which each part can be used while construction continues on other parts.

In accordance with IPSAS 5.16, the accounting treatment for borrowing costs must be disclosed in the financial statements.

Effective date

Periods beginning on or after 1 July 2001.

Proposed changes to IPSAS 5

In ED 35 "Borrowing Costs" published on 3 September 2008, the IPSASB proposed revising IPSAS 5. Diverging from the revised IAS 23, the IPSASB has taken the stance that borrowing costs should be expensed rather than capitalized as part of the cost of an asset without effect on surplus or deficit. It argues that borrowing costs should, if at all, only be eligible for capitalization if they were incurred specifically for the acquisition, construction or production of a qualifying asset (option).

The comment period of IPSAS ED 35 ended on 7 January 2009. The analysis of the responses by the IPSASB staff showed that roughly half of the respondents did not agree with the proposals in IPSAS ED 35. Therefore, the IPSASB concluded that there was no clear mandate to finalize IPSAS ED 35. In its Washington Meeting in May the IPSASB agreed to consider the issue further using the preliminary views developed in the measurement phase (Phase 3) of its Conceptual Framework project. It is likely that a decision on ED 35 will be postponed by the IPSASB as long as this work has not been completed.

IPSAS 6: Consolidated and Separate Financial Statements

Objective

The standard sets out requirements of the preparation and presentation of consolidated financial statements of an **economic entity** under the accrual basis of accounting. In addition, it contains guidance on the scope of a consolidated group of an economic entity and describes the consolidation procedures. It also presents rules on accounting for public sector subsidiaries, jointly controlled public sector entities and associates in separate financial statements.

The IFRS on which the IPSAS is based

IAS 27 "Consolidated and Separate Financial Statements"

Content

Principal definitions

Economic entity means a group of entities comprising a controlling entity (public sector parent) and one or more controlled entities (public sector subsidiaries).

Control is the power to govern the financial and operating policies of another entity so as to benefit from its activities.

The financial statements of an economic entity are referred to as **consolidated financial statements** under IPSASs. This is equivalent to the term used under IFRS.

Separate financial statements in accordance with IPSASs are financial statements presented by a controlling entity, an investor in an associate or a venturer in a jointly controlled entity, in which the investments are accounted for on the basis of the direct net assets/equity interest rather than on the basis of the reported results and net assets of the investees.

Duty to present consolidated financial statements

A controlling entity presents consolidated financial statements by consolidating its controlled entities in accordance with the provisions of this standard. It is exempted from the presentation of consolidated financial statements in accordance with IPSAS 6.16 if it satisfies all of the following criteria:

    (a)   The controlling entity is

        (i)   itself a wholly-owned controlled entity and users of consolidated financial statements of this entity are unlikely to exist or their information needs are met by its controlling entity's consolidated financial statements; or

        (ii) a partially-owned controlled entity of another entity and its other owners, including those not otherwise entitled to decide on the presentation of consolidated financial statements, have been informed about, and do not object to, such a decision.

    (b)   The controlling entity's debt or equity instruments are not traded in a public market.

    (c)   The controlling entity did not file, nor is it in the process of filing, its financial statements with a securities commission or other regulatory organization for the purpose of issuing any class of instruments in a public market.

    (d)   This controlling entity's ultimate or any intermediate controlling entity produces consolidated financial statements available for public use that comply with IPSASs.

If a controlling entity satisfies the exempting criteria, it may elect not to present consolidated financial statements and present only separate financial statements.

Scope of the consolidated group

Consolidated financial statements are generally required to include all public sector subsidiaries in the group of consolidated entities (cf. IPSAS 6.20). In accordance with IPSAS 6.21, the only exception to this rule are those controlled entities where control is created temporarily only because they are acquired and held exclusively for the purpose of disposal within 12 months of the acquisition date, and management is actively seeking a buyer. In this case, the entity concerned is classified as a financial instrument, and accounted for accordingly (cf. IPSAS 15).

The decisive criterion for consolidation of an entity is **control**. The assessment of whether an entity is controlled is made based on the above criteria of the definition of control. IPSAS 6.30 et seq. elaborates how control should be interpreted in the public sector and in which cases control exists for financial reporting purposes. Some examples are also given here. When examining the relationship between two entities, IPSAS 6.39 prescribes that control be assumed when one or more of the **power conditions** and one or more of the **benefit conditions** are satisfied, unless there is clear evidence that the entity in question is controlled by another entity. If one or more of the conditions for power and benefits listed in IPSAS 6.39 apply for the entities in question, the indicators listed in IPSAS 6.40 for **power** and **benefit** can be used to assess whether control exists.

Figure 4 "Determining the consolidated group for consolidated financial statements in accordance with IPSASs" below summarizes the procedure for determining the entities to be included in consolidated financial statements in accordance with IPSASs.

Consolidation procedures

In preparing consolidated financial statements, the financial statements of the controlling entities and its controlled entities are combined on a line-by-line basis by adding together similar or identical items of assets, liabilities, net assets/equity, revenue and expenses.

The financial statements of the controlling entity and its controlled entities used in the preparation of the consolidated financial statements are usually prepared as of the same reporting date. When the reporting dates of the controlling entity and a controlled entity are different, the controlled entity prepares interim financial statements as of the same date as the financial statements of the controlling entity unless it is impracticable to do so.

When the date of the financial statements of a controlled entity used in the preparation of consolidated financial statements differs from that of the controlling entity, adjustments are made for the effects of significant transactions or events that occur between that date and the date of the controlling entity's financial statements. The difference between the reporting date of the controlled entity and that of the controlling entity may not, however, be more than three months. The length of the reporting periods and any difference in the reporting dates must be the same from period to period.

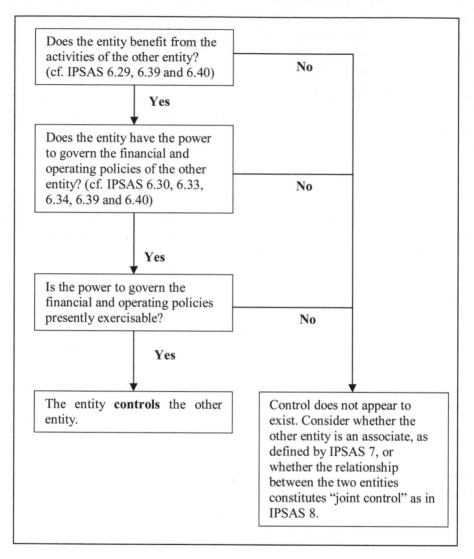

Figure 4:   *Determining the consolidated group for consolidated financial statements in accordance with IPSASs*

The following steps are required in order to make sure that the consolidated financial statements present financial information about the economic entity as if it were a single entity (cf. IPSAS 6.43):

(a) The carrying amount of the shares belonging to the controlling entity in each controlled entity and the controlling entity's share in the net assets/equity of each controlled entity are eliminated.

(b) Minority interests in the surplus or deficit of consolidated subsidiaries for the reporting period are identified separately.

(c) Minority interests in the net assets/equity of consolidated controlled entities are identified and presented in the consolidated statement of financial position separately from liabilities and the controlling entity's shareholders' net assets/equity. Minority interests in the net assets/equity consist of:

(i) the amount of the minority interests at the date of the original combination and

(ii) the share of changes in net assets/equity attributable to the minority interest since the date of the combination.

Intercompany balances, transactions and revenue and expenses between entities are eliminated in full in accordance with IPSAS 6.45. Consolidated financial statements must be prepared using uniform accounting policies for similar or identical transactions and other events in similar circumstances. Minority interests are presented in the consolidated statement of financial position within net assets/equity, separately from the controlling entity's net assets/equity. Minority interests in the surplus or deficit of the group are also disclosed separately.

Accounting for investments in subsidiaries, jointly controlled entities and associates in separate financial statements in accordance with IPSASs

IPSAS 6.58 provides for investments in subsidiaries, jointly controlled entities and associates to be accounted for in separate financial statements in accordance with IPSASs either

(a) using the equity method described in IPSAS 7,

(b) at cost, or

(c) as financial instruments.

The same accounting policies must be applied for each category of investments.

Subsidiaries, jointly controlled entities and associates that are accounted for as financial instruments in the consolidated financial statements are accounted for in the same way in the shareholder's separate financial statements.

Effective date

Periods beginning on or after 1 January 2008.

IPSAS 7: Investments in Associates

Objective

This standard governs the accounting for investments in associates where the investment in the associate takes the form of shares or other equity instruments, but does not cover investments in associates held by venture capital organizations or investment funds, unit trusts or similar entities such as investment-linked insurance funds. Such investments are measured at fair value with changes in fair value recognized in surplus or deficit in the period in accordance with relevant international or national accounting standards for the recognition and measurement of financial instruments.

The IFRS on which the IPSAS is based

IAS 28 "Investments in Associates"

Content

Principal definitions

An **associate** is an entity, including an unincorporated entity such as a partnership, over which the investor has **significant influence** and that is neither a controlled entity nor an interest in a joint venture (cf. IPSAS 8).

Separate financial statements in accordance with IPSASs are financial statements presented by a controlling entity, an investor in an associate or a venturer in a jointly controlled entity, in which the investments are accounted for on the basis of the direct net assets/equity interest rather than on the basis of the reported results and net assets of the investees. Financial statements of an entity that does not have a controlled entity (subsidiary), associate or venturer's interest in a joint venture are **not separate financial statements** in accordance with IPSASs.

Significant influence

Significant influence according to IPSAS 7.7 is the power to participate in the financial and operating policy decisions of the investee but is not control or joint control over those policies. The assessment of whether an investor has significant influence over the investee is judged based on the nature of the relationship. IPSAS 7.12 lists indicators that should be referred to for assessing whether an investor has significant influence.

The existence of significant influence is usually evidenced in one or more of the following ways:

65

- Representation on the board of directors or equivalent governing body of the investee
- Participation in policy-making processes, including participation in decisions about dividends or other distributions
- Material transactions between the investor and the investee
- Interchange of managerial personnel
- Provision of essential technical information

If a public-sector investor holds, directly or indirectly (e.g., through subsidiaries), 20% or more of the voting power of the investee, it is presumed that the investor does have significant influence, unless it can be clearly demonstrated that this is not the case. Conversely, if the investor holds less than 20% of the voting rights, directly or indirectly (e.g., through a subsidiary), it is presumed that the investor does not have significant influence unless such influence can be clearly demonstrated. A substantial or majority ownership by another investor does not necessarily preclude an investor from having significant influence.

Application of the equity method

Investments in associates are generally accounted for in the consolidated financial statements using the **equity method**. The equity method is a method of accounting whereby the investment is initially recognized at cost and subsequently adjusted for the post-acquisition change in the investor's share of net assets/equity of the investee. The surplus or deficit of the investor includes the investor's share of the surplus or deficit of the investee. Distributions received from an investee reduce the carrying amount of the investment. Adjustments to the carrying amount may also be necessary for changes in the investor's proportionate interest in the investee arising from changes in the investee's equity that have not been recognized in the investee's surplus or deficit. Such changes can arise from revaluation of property, plant and equipment (cf. IPSAS 17) or from translation of financial statements denominated in foreign currency (IPSAS 4). In contrast to the adjustments to the carrying amount for changes in the investor's proportionate interest, the investor's share of those changes is recognized directly in the investor's equity/net assets.

IPSAS 7.19 describes exceptional cases where an investee is not accounted for using the equity method. This is the case, for example, when investments are acquired with the aim of disposal within 12 months from the acquisition date and management is actively seeking a buyer. Such investments must be classified as "held for trading" and be accounted for in accordance with the applicable international or national accounting standards for the recognition and measurement of financial instruments.

As soon as an investor ceases to have significant influence over an associate, it discontinues the use of the equity method and accounts for the investment in accordance with the applicable international or national accounting standards for the recognition and measurement of financial instruments, provided the associate does not become a subsidiary or a joint venture as defined in IPSAS 8.

The carrying amount of the investment at the date that the investee ceases to be an associate is regarded as its cost on initial measurement as a financial asset in accordance with the applicable international or national accounting standards for the recognition and measurement of financial instruments.

In applying the equity method, the investor uses the most recent available financial statements of the associate (cf. IPSAS 7.30). When the reporting dates of the investor and the associate are different, the associate prepares, for the use of the investor, financial statements as of the same date as the financial statements of the investor unless it is impracticable to do so.

When the financial statements of an associate used in applying the equity method are prepared as of a different reporting date from that of the investor, adjustments must be made for the effects of significant transactions or events that occur between that date and the date of the investor's financial statements. In any case, the difference between the reporting date of the associate and that of the investor may not exceed three months. The length of the reporting periods and any difference in the reporting dates must be the same from period to period.

In accordance with IPSAS 7.32, the investor's financial statements are usually prepared using uniform accounting policies for similar or identical transactions and events in similar circumstances. If an associate uses accounting policies other than those of the investor for similar or identical transactions and events in similar circumstances, adjustments must be made to bring the associate's accounting policies in line with those of the investor.

Deficits of investments accounted for using the equity method

In the event that the associate sustains deficits on a permanent basis, the carrying amount of the investment would be negative as of a certain date if the investor continued recognizing its share of the deficits. For this reason, IPSAS 7.35 et seq. rules that the investor should not recognize any further share in deficits once the investor's share in an associate's deficits equals or exceeds its interest in the associate. The investment is thus reported at a value of nil. A separate record must be kept of any additional losses. If surpluses are generated subsequently, they are initially used to offset the share of deficits recorded separately. Only when they exceed the additional losses does the investor resume recognizing its share in the surplus in the carrying amount of the investment.

Determining impairment losses

After application of the equity method, including recognizing the associate's losses in accordance with IPSAS 7.35 et seq., the investor applies the requirements of the relevant international and national accounting standards dealing with the recognition and measurement of financial instruments to determine whether it is necessary to recognize any additional impairment loss with respect to the investor's net investment in the associate.

The investor also applies the requirements of the relevant international and national accounting standards to determine whether any additional impairment loss is recognized with respect to the investor's interest in the associate that does not constitute part of the net investment and the amount of the impairment loss.

Accounting for investments in associates in separate financial statements

In an investor's separate financial statements prepared under IPSASs, investments in associates are recognized in accordance with IPSAS 6.58-64 (cf. IPSAS 7.41).

Entities may prepare separate financial statements in accordance with IPSASs as their only set of financial statements if they are exempted in accordance with IPSAS 6.16 ("Consolidated and Separate Financial Statements") from consolidation or in accordance with IPSAS 8.3 ("Interests in Joint Ventures") from proportionate consolidation or in accordance with IPSAS 7.19(b) from application of the equity method.

Effective date

Periods beginning on or after 1 January 2008.

IPSAS 8: Interests in Joint Ventures

Objective

IPSAS 8 governs accounting for interests in joint ventures and the reporting of joint venture assets, liabilities, revenue and expenses in the financial statements of venturers and investors, regardless of the structures or forms under which the joint venture activities take place.

It does not apply to venturers' interests in jointly controlled entities held by (a) venture capital organizations or (b) investment funds, unit trusts or similar entities such as investment-linked insurance funds. Such investments are measured at fair value with changes in fair value recognized in surplus or deficit in the period in accordance with relevant international or national accounting standards for the recognition and measurement of financial instruments.

The IFRS on which the IPSAS is based

IAS 31 "Interests in Joint Ventures"

Content

Principal definitions

A **joint venture** is a binding arrangement whereby two or more parties are committed to undertake an activity that is subject to joint control. The binding arrangement may for example take the form of a contract. The arrangement usually specifies the original capital contribution and the sharing of revenue or other forms of consideration and expenses between the venturers.

Joint control is the agreed sharing of control over an activity by a binding arrangement. IPSAS 8.7 et seq. specifies what kinds of arrangements qualify as a binding arrangement.

A **venturer** is a party to a joint venture and has joint control over that joint venture. IPSAS 8 refers to the fact that joint ventures in the public sector may conduct commercial activities and/or provide community services at no charge.

An **investor** in a joint venture is a party to a joint venture and does not have joint control over that joint venture.

69

Forms and characteristics of joint ventures

In practice, **joint ventures** take many different forms and structures. IPSAS 8.11 et seq. identifies three broad types which are commonly described as joint ventures and meet the definition of joint ventures:

- **Jointly controlled operations**
- **Jointly controlled assets**
- **Jointly controlled entities**

Accounting for joint ventures

Different accounting treatments apply for each type of joint venture.

Jointly controlled operations (cf. IPSAS 8.19): For their interests in jointly controlled operations, venturers are required to recognize in their financial statements:

(a) The assets that they control and the liabilities that they incur

(b) The expenses that they incur and their share of the revenue that they earn from the sale or provision of goods or services by the joint venture

Jointly controlled assets (cf. IPSAS 8.25): For their interests in jointly controlled assets, venturers are required to recognize in their financial statements:

(a) Their share of the jointly controlled assets, classified according to the nature of the assets

(b) Any liabilities that they have incurred, for example for financing their share of the assets

(c) Their share of any liabilities incurred jointly with the other venturers in relation to the joint venture

(d) Any revenue from the sale or use of their share of the output of the joint venture, together with their share of any expenses incurred by the joint venture

(e) Any expenses that they have incurred in respect of their interest in the joint venture

Jointly controlled entities: There are two possible methods of consolidation:

(a) **Proportionate consolidation:** Proportionate consolidation is a method of accounting whereby a venturer's share of each of the assets, liabilities, revenue and expenses of a jointly controlled entity is combined line by line with similar items in the venturer's financial statements or reported as separate line items in the venturer's financial statements. A venturer should discontinue the use of proportionate consolidation from the date on which it ceases to have joint control over a jointly controlled entity.

(b) **Equity method** (also see the rules of IPSAS 7): A venturer should discontinue the use of the equity method from the date on which it ceases to have joint control over, or have significant influence in, a jointly controlled entity.

Like the IASB, the IPSASB recommends using the proportionate method of consolidation for jointly controlled entities because it better reflects the substance and economic reality of a venturer's interest in a jointly controlled entity (cf. IPSAS 8.37 and IPSAS 8.45).

Special aspects of accounting for joint ventures

Exceptions to proportionate consolidation and equity method

- When there is evidence that the interest in a joint venture has been acquired and is held exclusively with a view to its disposal within 12 months from acquisition and that management is actively seeking a buyer, the interest is classified as held for trading and accounted for in accordance with the relevant international or national accounting standard dealing with the recognition and measurement of financial instruments.

- The venturer must account for its interest in accordance with IPSAS 6 as of the date on which the jointly controlled entity becomes a subsidiary of the venturer. The venturer must account for its interest in accordance with IPSAS 7 as of the date on which the jointly controlled entity becomes an associate of the venturer.

IPSAS 6.54 et seq. describes the accounting treatment for transactions between a venturer and a joint venture in the financial statements.

In accordance with IPSAS 8.52, interests in jointly controlled entities are recognized in a venturer's separate financial statements in accordance with IPSAS 6.58-64.

An investor in a joint venture that does not have joint control, but does have significant influence is required to account for its interest in a joint venture in accordance with IPSAS 7.

Effective date

Periods beginning on or after 1 January 2008.

IPSAS 9: Revenue from Exchange Transactions

Objective

This standard prescribes the accounting treatment of revenue arising from exchange transactions and events, the main question being **when to recognize** revenue. Revenue is recognized when it is probable that future economic benefits or service potential will flow to the entity and these benefits can be measured reliably. IPSAS 9 identifies those circumstances in which these criteria are satisfied and when revenue needs to be recognized accordingly. It also provides practical guidance on the application of these criteria.

The IFRS on which the IPSAS is based

IAS 18 "Revenue"

Content

Principal definitions

Revenue is the gross inflow of economic benefits or service potential during the reporting period when those inflows result in an increase in net assets/equity, other than increases relating to contributions from owners.

Exchange transactions are transactions in which one entity receives assets or services, or has liabilities extinguished, and directly gives approximately equal value (primarily in the form of cash, goods, services, or use of assets) to another entity in exchange. Typical exchange transactions are the purchase or sale of goods or services based on market prices.

Non-exchange transactions are transactions that are not exchange transactions. In a non-exchange transaction, an entity either receives value from another entity without directly giving approximately equal value in exchange, or gives value to another entity without directly receiving approximately equal value in exchange. In the public sector, typical examples of revenue from non-exchange transactions are taxes and dues, transfers and donations (cf. IPSAS 23 for more details).

Application

IPSAS 9 applies to revenue arising from the following exchange transactions and events:

- The rendering of services
- The sale of goods
- The use by others of entity assets yielding interest, royalties and dividends

Certain specific items to be recognized as revenues are addressed in other standards and are therefore excluded from the scope of this standard. For example, gains arising on the sale of property, plant and equipment are specifically addressed in standards on property, plant and equipment and are therefore not covered in this standard.

Measurement of revenue

As in the private sector, revenue from exchange transactions is measured at the **fair value** of the consideration received or receivable taking into account the amount of any trade discounts and volume rebates allowed by the entity. In the case of long-term payment terms, IPSAS 9.16 stipulates that the present value of all future receipts be used as a basis.

Recognition of revenue from the rendering of services

When the outcome of a transaction involving the rendering of services can be estimated reliably, revenue associated with the transaction is recognized by reference to the stage of completion of the transaction at the reporting date (cf. IPSAS 9.19 et seq.). IPSAS 9.19 thus provides for recognition of the revenue according to the stage of completion, also referred to as the percentage of completion method. The stage of completion of a transaction can be determined in a variety of ways. IPSAS 9.23 instructs public sector entities to use the method that measures reliably the services performed. Depending on the nature of the transaction, the methods may include:

(a) Surveys of work performed

(b) Services performed to date as a percentage of total services to be performed

(c) The proportion that costs incurred to date bear to the estimated total costs of the transaction. Only costs that reflect services performed to date are included in costs incurred to date. Only costs that reflect services performed or to be performed are included in the estimated total costs of the transaction.

This list of methods given in IPSAS 9.23 is not exhaustive. IPSAS 9.23 also refers to the fact that progress payments and advances received from customers often do not reflect the services performed, i.e., the stage of completion cannot be inferred from them.

For practical purposes, IPSAS 9.24 allows revenue to be recognized on a straight-line basis over the specified time frame when services are performed in an indeterminate number of steps over a specified time frame, unless there is evidence that some other method better represents the stage of completion.

The **outcome of a transaction involving the rendering of services** can be estimated **reliably** only when all the following conditions are satisfied (cf. IPSAS 9.19):

(a) The amount of revenue can be measured reliably.

(b) It is probable that the economic benefits or service potential associated with the transaction will flow to the entity.

(c) The stage of completion of the transaction at the reporting date can be measured reliably (cf. IPSAS 9.22 for further details).

(d) The costs incurred for the transaction and the costs to complete the transaction can be measured reliably.

When the outcome of the transaction involving the rendering of services cannot be estimated reliably, revenue may be recognized in accordance with IPSAS 9.25 only to the extent of the expenses recognized that are recoverable.

Recognition of revenue from sale of goods

Revenue from the sale of goods is recognized when all the following conditions have been satisfied (cf. IPSAS 9.28):

(a) The entity has transferred to the purchaser the significant risks and rewards of ownership of the goods.

(b) The entity retains neither continuing managerial involvement to the degree usually associated with ownership nor effective control over the goods sold.

(c) The amount of revenue can be measured reliably.

(d) It is probable that the economic benefits associated with the transaction will flow to the entity.

(e) The costs incurred or to be incurred in respect of the transaction can be measured reliably.

The assessment of when an entity has transferred the significant risks and rewards of ownership to the purchaser requires an examination of the circumstances of the transaction in accordance with IPSAS 9.29. If the entity retains significant risks of ownership, the transaction does not constitute a sale and revenue is therefore not recognized. It is therefore possible that a public sector entity might retain significant risks of ownership in a number of different ways (e.g., by means of guarantees or collateral). If an entity retains only an insignificant risk of ownership, the transaction constitutes a sale and revenue is recognized (cf. IPSAS 9.31). Another key criterion regarding the reliability of revenue recognition is that an inflow of resources is probable. In some cases, this may not be probable until the consideration is received or until an uncertainty is removed. For example, a public sector entity's revenue may depend on the ability of another entity to supply goods on the basis of contractual arrangements (cf. example given in IPSAS 9.32). Should there be any doubt that this will occur, revenue is not realized until the doubt is eliminated. When goods have been supplied, the uncertainty is removed and revenue can be recognized.

Recognition of revenue from interest, royalties and dividends

Revenue from the use by others of entity assets – including interest, royalties and dividends in accordance with IPSAS 9.33 – is recognized when it is probable that the economic benefits or service potential associated with the transaction will flow to the entity and the amount of the revenue can be measured reliably. If the revenue meets these conditions, it is recognized as follows:

- Interest is recognized on a time proportion basis that takes into account the effective yield on the asset.
- Royalties are recognized as they are earned in accordance with the substance of the relevant agreement.
- Dividends or their equivalents are recognized when the shareholder's or the entity's right to receive payment is established.

The appendix to IPSAS 9 contains illustrative examples on determining when to recognize revenue from certain exchange transactions.

Effective date

Periods beginning on or after 1 July 2002; earlier application is encouraged.

IPSAS 10: Financial Reporting in Hyperinflationary Economies

Objective

IPSAS 10 governs financial statements of public sector entities whose functional currency (cf. IPSAS 4.11 et seq.) is the currency of a hyperinflationary economy. In a hyperinflationary economy, financial reporting in the local currency without restatement is not useful. Money loses purchasing power at such a rate that comparison of amounts from transactions and other events that have occurred at different times, even within the same reporting period, is misleading.

The IFRS on which the IPSAS is based

IAS 29 "Financial Reporting in Hyperinflationary Economies"

Content

Principal definitions

Functional currency is the currency of the primary economic environment in which the entity operates. The primary economic environment of an entity is normally the one in which it primarily generates and expends cash.

Presentation currency is the currency in which the financial statements are presented.

Monetary items are money held and assets and liabilities to be received or paid in fixed or determinable amounts of money.

Application

IPSAS 10 applies to the primary financial statements, including the consolidated financial statements, of any entity whose functional currency is the currency of a hyperinflationary economy.

IPSAS 10 does not establish an absolute rate at which hyperinflation is deemed to exist. When restatement of financial statements in accordance with this standard becomes necessary is a matter of judgment. Hyperinflation is indicated by characteristics of the economic environment of a country which include, but are not limited to, the list given in IPSAS 10.4.

Recognition

The financial statements of an entity that reports in the currency of a hyperinflationary economy should be stated in terms of the measuring unit current at the reporting date. The comparative figures for the previous period required by IPSAS 1 "Presentation of Financial Statements" and any information in respect of earlier periods must also be stated in terms of the measuring unit current at the reporting date. For the purpose of presenting comparative amounts in a different presentation currency, cf. IPSAS 4.47 (b) and IPSAS 4.48. The surplus or deficit on the net monetary position must be included in the surplus or deficit for the period and be disclosed separately in the statement of financial performance.

The restatement of financial statements in accordance with IPSAS 10 (e.g., by applying a general price index) requires the application of certain procedures as well as judgment. The consistent application of these procedures and judgments from period to period is more important than the precise accuracy of the resulting amounts included in the restated financial statements.

When an economy ceases to be hyperinflationary and an entity discontinues the preparation and presentation of financial statements prepared in accordance with this standard, it is required to treat the amounts expressed in the measuring unit current at the end of the previous reporting period as the basis for the carrying amounts in its subsequent financial statements.

Effective date

Periods beginning on or after 1 July 2002.

Objective

IPSAS 11 regulates the accounting treatment of revenue and costs associated with construction contracts in the financial statements of public sector entities acting as contractor under such contract. The standard

- Identifies the arrangements that are to be classified as construction contracts
- Provides guidance on the types of construction contracts that can arise in the public sector
- Specifies the basis for recognition and disclosure of contract expenses and, if relevant, contract revenues

Because of the nature of the activity undertaken in construction contracts, the date at which the contract activity is entered into and the date when the activity is completed usually fall into different reporting periods.

In many jurisdictions, construction contracts entered into by public sector entities will not specify an amount of contract revenue. Rather, funding to support the construction activity will be provided by an appropriation or similar allocation of general government revenue, or by aid or grant funds. In these cases, the primary issue in accounting for construction contracts is the allocation of construction costs to the reporting period in which the construction work is performed and the recognition of related expenses.

In some jurisdictions, construction contracts entered into by public sector entities may be established on a commercial basis or a non-commercial full or partial cost recovery basis. In these cases, the primary issue in accounting for construction contracts is the allocation of both contract revenue and contract costs to the reporting periods in which construction work is performed.

The IFRS on which the IPSAS is based

IAS 11 "Construction Contracts"

Principal definitions

A **construction contract** is a contract, or a similar binding arrangement, specifically negotiated for the construction of an asset or a combination of assets that are closely interrelated or interdependent in terms of their design, technology and function or their ultimate purpose or use (cf. IPSAS 11.4 and for more detail IPSAS 11.5 et seq.).

IPSAS 11 essentially distinguishes between **fixed price contracts** and **cost plus contracts** (cf. IPSAS 11.8 et seq.). A **fixed price contract** is a construction contract in which the contractor agrees to a fixed contract price, or a fixed rate per unit of output, which in some cases is subject to cost escalation clauses. A **cost plus contract** is a construction contract in which the contractor is reimbursed for allowable or otherwise defined costs and, in the case of a commercially-based contract, an additional percentage of these costs or a fixed fee, if any. In practice, the distinction might not always be that straight-forward.

General remark

IPSAS 11 governs the accounting for construction contracts for those rare cases in the public sector where a public sector entity acts as contractor. It is much more frequent for public sector entities to assume the position of principal, for example in a public invitation to tender.

Application

The requirements of IPSAS 11 are usually applied separately to each construction contract. However, in certain circumstances, it is necessary to apply the standard to the separately identifiable components of a single contract or to a group of contracts together in order to reflect the substance of a contract or a group of contracts.

If a contract covers a number of assets, the construction of each asset should be treated as a separate construction contract when the conditions set forth in IPSAS 11.13 are satisfied.

In certain cases, a group of contracts, whether with a single customer or with several customers, needs to be treated as a single construction contract. For further details, cf. IPSAS 11.14.

A contract may provide for the construction of an additional asset at the option of the customer or may be amended to include the construction of an additional asset. The construction of the additional asset is treated as a

80

separate construction contract provided the conditions listed in IPSAS 11.15 are satisfied.

Contract revenue and contract costs

Contract revenue comprises (cf. IPSAS 11.16):

(a) The initial amount of revenue agreed in the contract

(b) Variations in contract work, claims and incentive payments

  (i) to the extent that it is probable that they will result in revenue and

  (ii) they are capable of being reliably measured.

Contract revenue is measured at the **fair value** of the consideration received or receivable.

Contract costs comprise (cf. IPSAS 11.23):

(a) Costs that relate directly to the specific contract (cf. IPSAS 11.24 et seq. for details)

(b) Costs that may be attributable to contract activity in general and can be allocated to the specific contracts (cf. IPSAS 11.26 for details)

(c) Such other costs that are specifically chargeable to the customer under the terms of the contract (cf. IPSAS 11.27)

Costs that cannot be attributed to contract activity or cannot be allocated to a contract are excluded from the costs of a construction contract. Such costs include (cf. IPSAS 11.28):

(a) General administration costs for which reimbursement is not specified in the contract

(b) Selling costs

(c) Research and development costs for which reimbursement is not specified in the contract

(d) Depreciation of idle plant and equipment that is not used on a particular contract

Recognition

When the outcome of a construction contract can be estimated reliably, contract revenue and contract costs associated with the construction contract are recognized as revenue and expenses respectively by reference to the **stage of completion** of the contract activity at the reporting date. An expected deficit on the construction contract is recognized as an expense immediately in accordance with IPSAS 11.44. The recognition of revenue and expenses by reference to the stage of completion of a contract is often referred to as the percentage of completion method.

In the case of a **fixed price contract**, the outcome of a construction contract can be estimated reliably when all the following conditions are satisfied (cf. IPSAS 11.31):

(a) Total contract revenue, if any, can be measured reliably

(b) It is probable that the economic benefits or service potential associated with the contract will flow to the entity

(c) Both the contract costs to complete the contract and the stage of contract completion at the reporting date can be measured reliably

(d) The contract costs attributable to the contract can be clearly identified and measured reliably so that actual contract costs incurred can be compared with prior estimates

In the case of a **cost plus contract**, the outcome of a construction contract can be estimated reliably when all the following conditions are satisfied (cf. IPSAS 11.32):

(a) It is probable that the economic benefits or service potential associated with the contract will flow to the entity

(b) The contract costs attributable to the contract, whether or not specifically reimbursable, can be clearly identified and measured reliably

The **stage of completion of a contract** may be determined in a variety of ways. Public sector entities should use the method that measures reliably the work performed. Depending on the nature of the contract, the methods may include (cf. IPSAS 11.38):

(a) The proportion that contract costs incurred for work performed to date bear to the estimated total contract costs

(b) Surveys of work performed

(c) Completion of a physical proportion of the contract work

When the outcome of a construction contract cannot be measured reliably, revenue is recognized only to the extent of contract costs incurred that it is probable will be recoverable. The contract costs are recognized as an expense in the period in which they are incurred. An expected deficit on the construction contract is recognized as an expense immediately in accordance with IPSAS 11.44.

The percentage of completion method is applied on a cumulative basis in each reporting period to the current estimates of contract revenue and contract costs. Therefore, the effect of a change in the estimate of contract revenue or contract costs, or the effect of a change in the estimate of the outcome of a contract, is accounted for as a change in accounting estimate (cf. IPSAS 3, "Accounting Policies, Changes in Accounting Estimates and Errors"). The changed estimates are used when determining the amount of revenue and expenses recognized in the statement of financial performance in the period in which the change is made and in subsequent periods.

Effective date

Periods beginning on or after 1 July 2002.

IPSAS 12: Inventories

Objective

The objective of this standard is to prescribe the accounting treatment for inventories. A primary issue in accounting for inventories is the amount of cost to be recognized as an asset and carried forward until the related revenues are recognized. This standard provides guidance on the determination of cost and its subsequent recognition as an expense, including any write-down to net realizable value. It also provides guidance on the cost formulas that are used to assign costs to inventories.

The IFRS on which the IPSAS is based

IAS 2 "Inventories"

Content

Principal definitions

In accordance with IPSAS 12.9, **inventories** are assets

    (a) In the form of materials and supplies to be consumed in the production process

    (b) In the form of materials or supplies to be consumed or distributed in the rendering of services

    (c) Held for sale or distribution in the ordinary course of business

    (d) In the process of production for sale or distribution

Inventories include goods purchased for resale, such as merchandise purchased by a retailer and held for resale or land and other property held for resale. In addition, inventories encompass finished goods produced or work in progress being produced and include materials and supplies awaiting use in the production process. Specifically in the public sector, inventories also comprise goods purchased or produced by the entity that are distributed to third parties for no charge or for a nominal charge. An example would be children's books produced by a ministry of family affairs for donation to schools.

Other examples of inventories in the public sector given in IPSAS 12.12 include: ammunition, maintenance materials, spare parts, strategic stockpiles (e.g., energy reserves or medicine), stocks of unissued currency, stamps, work in progress and property held for sale.

Net realizable value is the estimated selling price in the ordinary course of operations less the estimated costs of completion and the estimated costs necessary to make the sale, exchange or distribution.

Application

IPSAS 12 applies for all inventories except for:

(a) Work in progress arising under construction contracts, including directly related service contracts (cf. IPSAS 11 "Construction Contracts")

(b) Financial instruments

(c) Biological assets related to agricultural activity and agricultural produce at the point of harvest (cf. the relevant international or national accounting standard dealing with agriculture, e.g., IAS 41)

(d) Work in progress of services to be provided for no or nominal consideration

IPSAS 12 does not apply for the measurement of the following inventories:

(a) Producers' inventories of agricultural and forest products, agricultural produce after harvest, and minerals and mineral products, to the extent that they are measured at net realizable value in accordance with well-established practices in certain industries. When such inventories are measured at net realizable value, changes in that value are recognized in surplus or deficit in the period of the change.

(b) Inventories of commodity broker-traders who measure their inventories at fair value less costs to sell. When such inventories are measured at fair value less cost to sell, changes in that value are recognized in surplus or deficit in the period of the change.

Measurement of inventories

Inventories are required to be measured at the lower of **cost** and **net realizable value** (cf. IPSAS 12.15, for the basic measurement principles under IPSASs see Chapter I. 3).

Inventories acquired through a non-exchange transaction are measured at their **fair value** as of the date of acquisition (cf. IPSAS 12.16).

In contrast, inventories

• held for distribution at no charge or for a nominal charge

- held for consumption in the production process of goods to be distributed at no charge or for a nominal charge

are measured at the lower of **cost** and **current replacement cost** (cf. IPSAS 12.17).

The cost of inventories comprises all costs of purchase, costs of conversion and other costs incurred in bringing the inventories to their present location and condition (cf. IPSAS 12.18).

The costs of purchase of inventories comprise the purchase price, import duties and other taxes (other than those subsequently recoverable by the entity from the taxing authorities), and transport, handling and other costs directly attributable to the acquisition of finished goods, materials and supplies. Trade discounts, rebates and other similar items are deducted in determining the costs of purchase. The costs of conversion of inventories under IPSAS 12.20 et seq. include full production-related costs. The basis for determining costs of conversion is presented in IPSAS 12.20-23 (costs of conversion) and IPSAS 12.24-26 (other costs). The formula for calculating the costs of conversion of inventories is as follows:

	Direct costs
+	Fixed production overheads
+	Variable production overheads
+	Other costs
	Costs of conversion

Table 15: Calculating costs of conversion for inventories

In accordance with IPSAS 12.32 et seq., inventories are measured by applying the principle of specific identification according to which assets are measured individually. In the course of subsequent measurement, public sector entities have to review the existing inventories to ascertain whether their cost is recoverable or not, e.g. due to damage, if the inventories have become wholly or partially obsolete, or if their selling prices have declined. For this purpose, the net realizable value as of the reporting date must be determined (cf. IPSAS 12.38 et seq.). Inventories are usually written down to net realizable value item by item. However, according to IPSAS 12.39, in some circumstances it may be appropriate to group similar or related items together.

Simplified measurement methods

In accordance with IPSAS 12.32 et seq., inventories are generally measured individually. However, when inventories are stored, they may not be kept strictly separate and with prices fluctuating over time it is frequently impracticable to determine which portion of the asset or which assets have already been consumed and which are still in stock. If, however, there are a large number of inventories and they are ordinarily interchangeable, simplified measurement methods may be applied (cf. IPSAS 12.33 et seq.). If these conditions are satisfied, the costs of purchase or conversion of inventories are calculated by using the first-in, first-out (FIFO) or weighted average cost formulas. For all inventories of a similar nature and use to the entity, public sector entities must use the same cost formula. For inventories with a different nature or use, different cost formulas may be justifiable. This does not apply for inventories that are ordinarily not interchangeable and such goods, commodities or services produced and segregated for specific projects (cf. IPSAS 12.33).

Recognition of expenses relating to inventories

When inventories are sold, exchanged or distributed, the carrying amounts of those inventories are recognized as an expense in the period in which the related revenue is recognized (cf. IPSAS 12.44). If there is no related revenue, the expense is recognized when the goods are distributed or related service is rendered. The amount of any write-down of inventories and all losses of inventories are required to be recognized as an expense in the period the write-down or loss occurs. Any reversal of a write-down of inventories is deducted from the inventories recognized as an expense in the period in which the reversal occurs.

The disclosures in the notes required in relation to inventories are set forth in IPSAS 12.47 et seq.

Effective date

Periods beginning on or after 1 January 2008.

IPSAS 13: Leases

Objective

The objective of this standard is to prescribe, for **lessees** and **lessors**, the appropriate accounting policies and disclosures to apply in relation to **finance** and **operating leases**.

The IFRS on which the IPSAS is based

IAS 17 "Leases"

Content

Principal definitions

A **lease** is an agreement whereby the lessor conveys to the lessee in return for a payment or series of payments the right to use an asset for an agreed period of time.

A **finance lease** is a lease that transfers substantially all the risks and rewards incident to ownership of an asset. Title may or may not eventually be transferred. All other leases are **operating leases**. Operating leases do not transfer substantially all the risks and rewards incident to ownership of an asset.

Minimum lease payments are the payments over the lease term that the lessee is, or can be, required to make, excluding contingent rent, costs for services and, where appropriate, taxes to be paid by and reimbursed to the lessor, together with:

(a) For a lessee, any amounts guaranteed by the lessee or by a party related to the lessee

(b) For a lessor, any residual value guaranteed to the lessor by:

(i) The lessee

(ii) A party related to the lessee

(iii) An independent third party unrelated to the lessor that is financially capable of discharging the obligations under the guarantee

However, if the lessee has an option to purchase the asset at a price that is expected to be sufficiently lower than the fair value at the date the option becomes exercisable for it to be reasonably certain, at the inception of the lease, that the option will be exercised, then the result will be different. In this case the minimum lease payments comprise the minimum payments payable over the lease term to the expected date of exercise of this purchase option and the payment required to exercise it.

Scope

IPSAS 13 should be applied in accounting for all leases other than:

(a) Leases to explore for or use minerals, oil, natural gas and similar non-regenerative sources

(b) Licensing agreements for such items as motion picture films, video recordings, plays, manuscripts, patents and copyrights

IPSAS 13 is not applied as the basis of measurement for:

(a) Property held by lessees that is accounted for as investment property (cf. IPSAS 16, "Investment Property")

(b) Investment property provided by lessors under operating leases (cf. IPSAS 16)

(c) Biological assets held by lessees under finance leases (see the relevant international or national accounting standard dealing with agriculture)

(d) Biological assets held by lessors under operating leases (see the relevant international or national accounting standard dealing with agriculture)

Distinction between finance and operating leases

Whether a lease is a finance lease or an operating lease depends on the substance of the transaction rather than the form of the contract (cf. IPSAS 13.15). The following are examples of situations that individually or in combination would normally lead to a lease being classified as a finance lease:

(a) The lease transfers ownership of the asset to the lessee by the end of the lease term.

(b) The lessee has the option to purchase the asset at a price that is expected to be sufficiently lower than the fair value at the date the option becomes exercisable for it to be reasonably certain, at the inception of the lease, that the option will be exercised.

(c) The lease term is for the major part of the economic life of the asset even if title is not transferred.

    (d) At the inception of the lease the present value of the minimum lease payments amounts to at least substantially all of the fair value of the leased asset.

    (e) The leased assets are of such a specialized nature that only the lessee can use them without major modifications.

    (f) The leased assets cannot easily be replaced by another asset.

According to IPSAS 13.16, other indicators that individually or in combination could also lead to a lease being classified as a finance lease are:

    (a) If the lessee can cancel the lease, the lessor's losses associated with the cancellation are borne by the lessee.

    (b) Gains or losses from the fluctuation in the fair value of the residual accrue to the lessee (for example in the form of a rent rebate equaling most of the sales proceeds at the end of the lease).

    (c) The lessee has the ability to continue the lease for a secondary period at a rent that is substantially lower than market rent.

Pursuant to IPSAS 13.20, the land and buildings elements of a lease of land and buildings are considered separately for the purposes of lease classification.

Accounting for leases in the financial statements of lessees

a) Finance leases

At the commencement of the lease term lessees must recognize assets acquired under finance leases as assets and the associated lease obligations as liabilities in their statements of financial position (cf. IPSAS 13.28). The assets and liabilities are recognized at amounts equal to the fair value of the leased property or, if lower, the present value of the minimum lease payments, each determined at the inception of the lease. The discount rate to be used in calculating the present value of the minimum lease payments is the interest rate implicit in the lease, if this is practicable to determine. If not, the lessee's incremental borrowing rate must be used. In addition, the revenue from the lease should be distributed over the term of the lease in the same way as the depreciation and financing of a purchased asset (IPSAS 13.29).

Minimum lease payments are apportioned between the finance charge and the reduction of the outstanding liability (cf. IPSAS 13.34). The finance charge must be allocated to each period during the lease term so as to produce a constant periodic rate of interest on the remaining balance of the liability.

Contingent rents must be charged as expenses in the period in which they are incurred.

A finance lease gives rise to a depreciation expense for depreciable assets as well as the aforementioned finance charge for each accounting period. The depreciation policy for depreciable leased assets must be consistent with that for depreciable assets that are owned, and the depreciation recognized must be calculated in accordance with IPSAS 17 "Property, Plant and Equipment" and any international and/or national accounting standard on intangible assets which has been adopted by the entity. If there is no reasonable certainty that the lessee will obtain ownership by the end of the lease term, the asset must be fully depreciated over the shorter of the lease term or its useful life.

b) Operating leases

Lease payments under an operating lease must be recognized as an expense on a straight-line basis over the lease term unless another systematic basis is representative of the time pattern of the user's benefit.

Leases in the financial statements of lessors

a) Finance leases

A finance lease is a lease that transfers substantially all the risks and rewards incidental to ownership of an asset from the lessor to the lessee. In line with the assumption that the leased asset is purchased by the lessee, the lessor does not recognize the leased asset itself. In accordance with IPSAS 13.48, lessors must recognize lease payments receivable under a finance lease as assets in their statements of financial position and as a receivable at an amount equal to the net investment in the lease. The lessor recognizes as an asset in surplus or deficit a receivable for the payments expected in connection with the lease.

The result from the lease for the lessor is the **unearned finance revenue** that the lessor must distribute over the term of the lease. Unearned finance revenue is the total of the payments by the lessee (gross investment) and the fair value of the leased asset (net investment). IPSAS 13.51 provides that recognition of finance revenue should be based on a pattern reflecting a constant periodic rate of return on the lessor's net investment in the finance lease.

If artificially low rates of interest are quoted, any gains or losses on sale of assets must be restricted to that which would apply if a market rate of interest were charged.

b) Operating leases

Lessors must present assets subject to operating leases in their statements of financial position according to the nature of the asset.

Lease revenue from operating leases must be recognized as revenue on a straight-line basis over the lease term, unless another systematic basis is more representative of the time pattern in which benefits derived from the leased asset are diminished.

Initial direct costs incurred by lessors in negotiating and arranging an operating lease are added to the carrying amount of the leased asset and recognized as an expense over the lease term on the same basis as the lease revenue.

The depreciation policy for depreciable leased assets must be consistent with the lessor's normal depreciation policy for similar assets. Depreciation must be calculated in accordance with IPSAS 17, and any international and/or national accounting standard on intangible assets that has been adopted by the entity.

Accounting for sale and leaseback transactions

The accounting treatment of a sale and leaseback transaction depends mainly on whether the lease is a finance or an operating lease.

If a sale and leaseback transaction results in a finance lease, any excess of sales proceeds over the carrying amount cannot be immediately recognized as revenue by a seller-lessee. Instead, it must be deferred and amortized over the lease term.

If a sale and leaseback transaction results in an operating lease, and it is clear that the transaction is established at fair value, any gain or loss must be recognized immediately. Losses must be deferred if they are compensated by future lease payments below market price. If the sale price is above fair value, the excess over fair value is deferred and amortized over the period for which the asset is expected to be used. If the fair value is less than the carrying amount, any loss must be recognized immediately.

Effective date

Periods beginning on or after 1 January 2008.

IPSAS 14: Events after the Reporting Date

Objective

The objective of IPSAS 14 is to prescribe:

> (a) When an entity should adjust its financial statements for events after the reporting date
>
> (b) The disclosures that an entity should give about the date when the financial statements were authorized for issue and about events after the reporting date

The standard also requires that an entity should not prepare its financial statements on a going concern basis if events after the reporting date indicate that the going concern assumption is not appropriate (IPSAS 14.1).

The IFRS on which the IPSAS is based

IAS 10 "Events after the Balance Sheet Date"

Content

Principal definitions

Events after the reporting date are those events that occur between the reporting date and the date when the financial statements are authorized for issue. These events can be favorable and unfavorable for an entity.

Reporting date means the date of the last day of the reporting period to which the financial statements relate.

IPSAS 14.5 distinguishes between two types of events:

> (a) Events after the reporting date that provide evidence of conditions that existed at the reporting date (adjusting events after the reporting date)
>
> (b) Events after the reporting date that are indicative of conditions that arose after the balance sheet date (non-adjusting events after the reporting date)

In order to determine which events satisfy the definition of events after the reporting date, it is necessary to identify both the reporting date and the date on which the financial statements are authorized for issue. The **date of authorization for issue** is the date on which the financial statements have received approval from the individual or body with the authority to finalize those statements for issue. This can be a parliament or a local council (cf. IPSAS 14.7). IPSAS 14.8 points out that the date of authorization for issue of the financial statements will be determined in the context of the particular jurisdiction. The audit opinion is rendered on the basis of these financial statements.

In the period between the reporting date and the date of authorization for issue, elected government officials may announce a government's intentions in relation to certain matters (cf. IPSAS 14.9). Whether or not these announced government intentions require recognition as adjusting events would depend upon whether they provide more information about the conditions existing at the reporting date and whether there is sufficient evidence that they can and will be fulfilled. In most cases, the announcement of government intentions will not lead to the recognition of adjusting events. Instead, they would generally qualify for disclosure as non-adjusting events.

Accounting treatment of events after the reporting date

According to IPSAS 14.10, an entity must adjust the amounts recognized in its financial statements to reflect **adjusting events after the reporting date**. An example of an adjusting event after the reporting date could be the settlement after the reporting date of a court case, confirming that the entity had a present obligation at the reporting date. The entity adjusts any previously recognized provision related to this court case in accordance with IPSAS 19, "Provisions, Contingent Liabilities and Contingent Assets" or recognizes a new provision. The receipt of information after the reporting date indicating that an asset was impaired at the reporting date, or that the amount of a previously recognized impairment loss for that asset needs to be adjusted, also qualifies as an adjusting event after the reporting date. This is why the bankruptcy of a debtor which occurs after the reporting date usually confirms that a loss already existed at the reporting date on a receivable account and that the entity needs to adjust the carrying amount of the receivable account.

According to IPSAS 14.12 an entity cannot adjust the amounts recognized in its financial statements to reflect **non-adjusting events after the reporting date.** For example, in the event that an entity generally measures its land at fair value pursuant to IPSAS 17.44, a drop in the fair value of the land between the reporting date and the date of authorization for issue does not lead to any adjustments. The drop in the fair value of the land generally had nothing to do with its condition on the reporting date. Instead, it reflects the change in circumstances in the subsequent reporting period.

In the notes, an entity must disclose the following information for each material category of non-adjusting event after the reporting date:

- The nature of the event
- An estimate of its financial effect or a statement that such an estimate cannot be made

Going concern

The determination of whether the going concern assumption is appropriate needs to be considered by each entity. In the public sector, however, the assessment of going concern is likely to be of more relevance for individual entities (e.g., for local authorities) than for a government as a whole. For example, a government can decide to transfer the activities of one entity to another government agency. This could influence the going concern assumption for the transferring entity and its accounting.

According to IPSAS 14.18, an entity cannot prepare its financial statements on a going concern basis if those responsible for the preparation of the financial statements or the governing body determine after the reporting date either that there is an intention to liquidate the entity or to cease operating, or that there is no realistic alternative to this course of action.

In the case of entities whose operations are substantially budget-funded, going concern issues generally only arise if the government announces its intention to cease funding the entity (cf. IPSAS 14.20).

If the going concern assumption is no longer appropriate, IPSAS 14.22 provides that an entity must reflect this in its financial statements. Judgment is required in determining whether a change in the carrying amount of assets and liabilities is required, or whether additional liabilities have to be created (cf. IPSAS 14.22 et seq.). When the going concern assumption is no longer appropriate, effects on the maturity and classification of liabilities (e.g., due to contractual provisions that render liabilities due immediately in certain cases) may occur.

Other disclosure obligations

IPSAS 14.26 states that an entity must disclose the date when the financial statements were authorized for issue and who gave that authorization. If another body has the power to amend the financial statements after issuance, the entity must disclose that fact.

Effective date

Periods beginning on or after 1 January 2008.

IPSAS 15: Financial Instruments: Disclosure and Presentation

Objective

The dynamic nature of international financial markets has resulted in the widespread use of a variety of financial instruments ranging from traditional primary instruments, such as bonds, to various forms of derivative instruments, such as interest rate swaps. Public sector entities use a wide range of financial instruments from simple instruments such as payables and receivables to more complex instruments (such as cross-currency swaps to hedge commitments in foreign currencies) in their operations. To a lesser extent, public sector entities may issue equity instruments or compound liability/equity instruments. This may occur where an economic entity includes a partly-privatized Government Business Enterprise (GBE) that issues equity instruments into the financial markets or where a public sector entity issues debt instruments that convert to an ownership interest under certain conditions.

The objective of this standard is to enhance financial statement users' understanding of the significance of recognized and unrecognized financial instruments to a government's or other public sector entity's financial position, performance and cash flows.

IPSAS 15 prescribes certain requirements for presentation of on-balance-sheet financial instruments and identifies the information that should be disclosed about both on-balance-sheet (recognized) and off-balance-sheet (unrecognized) financial instruments. The **presentation rules** deal with the classification of financial instruments between liabilities and net assets/equity, the classification of related interest, dividends, revenues and expenses, and the circumstances in which financial assets and financial liabilities should be offset. The **disclosure rules** deal with information about factors that affect the amount, timing and certainty of an entity's future cash flows relating to financial instruments and the accounting policies applied to the instruments. In addition, IPSAS 15 encourages disclosure of information about the nature and extent of an entity's use of financial instruments, the financial purposes that they serve, the risks associated with them and management's policies for controlling those risks.

The IFRS on which the IPSAS is based

IPSAS 15 is mainly based on IAS 32 "Financial Instruments: Presentation". Accounting for financial instruments under IFRS is dealt with in IAS 32, of which the disclosures part has been replaced by IFRS 7 "Financial Instruments: Disclosures" since 2007, and in IAS 39 "Financial Instruments: Recognition and Measurement".

Because IPSAS 15 is based on IAS 32, it mainly deals with a distinction between net assets/equity and liabilities, possibilities of offsetting financial assets and liabilities as well as disclosure requirements in relation to financial instruments. Currently, IPSAS does not yet have an equivalent to IAS 39 that governs the recognition and measurement of financial instruments (see also our remarks at the end of the summary of IPSAS 15).

Content

Principal definitions

In accordance with IPSAS 15.9, a **financial instrument** is any contract that gives rise to both a financial asset of one entity and a financial liability or equity instrument of another entity.

A **financial asset** is any asset that is:

(a) Cash

(b) A contractual right to receive cash or another financial asset from another entity (e.g., bonds held)

(c) A contractual right to exchange financial instruments with another entity under conditions that are potentially favorable (e.g., a forward purchase of foreign currency at a forward rate that is below the spot rate)

(d) An equity instrument (e.g., shares) of another entity

A **financial liability** is any liability that is a contractual obligation:

(a) To deliver cash or another financial asset to another entity (e.g., bonds issued)

(b) To exchange financial instruments with another entity under conditions that are potentially unfavorable (e.g., the writer obligation for an option)

An **equity instrument** is any contract that evidences a residual interest in the assets of an entity after deducting all of its liabilities (e.g., shares).

Financial instruments thus comprise both **primary instruments** such as receivables, liabilities or equity securities, and **derivative financial instruments** such as futures or forwards, options or swaps (e.g., interest swaps).

Presentation of debts and net assets/equity

According to IPSAS 15.22, the issuer of a financial instrument should classify the instrument, or its component parts, as a liability or as net assets/equity in accordance with the substance of the contractual arrangement on initial recognition and the definitions of a financial liability and an equity instrument. The issuer of a financial instrument that comprises both a liability and a net assets/equity component must classify the two components separately and in accordance with IPSAS 15.22 (cf. IPSAS 15.29).

Interest, dividends, losses and gains relating to a financial instrument, or a component, classified as a financial liability should be reported in the statement of financial performance as expense or revenue. Distributions to holders of a financial instrument classified as an equity instrument should be debited by the issuer directly to net assets/equity.

Offsetting of a financial asset and a financial liability

A financial asset and a financial liability should be offset and the net amount reported in the statement of financial position (cf. IPSAS 15.39) when an entity:

(a) Has a legally enforceable right to set off the recognized amounts

(b) Intends either to settle on a net basis, or to realize the asset and settle the liability simultaneously

Disclosure requirements

In particular an entity should describe its financial risk management **objectives** and **policies**, including its policy for hedging each major type of forecasted transaction for which hedge accounting is used.

For each class of financial assets, financial liabilities and equity instruments, both recognized and unrecognized, an entity should disclose (cf. IPSAS 15.54):

(a) Information about the extent and nature of the financial instruments, including significant terms and conditions that may affect the amount, timing and certainty of future cash flows

    (b)   The accounting policies and methods adopted, including the criteria for recognition and the basis of measurement applied

Disclosures on the **interest rate risk** are also required. For each class of financial asset and financial liability, both recognized and unrecognized, an entity should disclose information about its exposure to interest rate risk (cf. IPSAS 15.63), including:

    (a)   Contractual repricing or maturity dates, whichever dates are earlier

    (b)   Effective interest rates, when applicable

For each class of financial asset, both recognized and unrecognized, an entity should disclose information about its exposure to **credit risk** (cf. IPSAS 15.73), including:

    (a)   The amount that best represents its maximum credit risk exposure at the reporting date, in the event of other parties failing to perform their obligations under financial instruments. The fair value of collateral is not considered here

    (b)   Significant concentrations of credit risk

For each class of financial assets and financial liabilities, both recognized and unrecognized, an entity should disclose information about the **fair value**. When it is not practicable within constraints of timeliness or cost to determine the fair value of a financial asset or financial liability with sufficient reliability, that fact should be disclosed together with information about the principal characteristics of the underlying financial instrument that are pertinent to its fair value.

IPSAS 15 contains disclosures in addition to the disclosure requirements stated here.

Effective date

Periods beginning on or after 1 January 2003.

Proposed changes on IPSAS 15:

IPSAS 15 was issued in December 2001 and was drawn primarily from IAS 32 (revised 1998). Since then the IASB has issued revised standards on financial instruments. In April 2009 the IPSASB published IPSAS ED 37 "Financial Instruments: Presentation", IPSAS ED 38 "Financial Instruments: Recognition and Measurement" and IPSAS ED 39 "Financial Instruments: Disclosures" as an integrated package. The EDs propose IPSASs that converge with the IASB's standards for financial instruments as at 31 December 2008, with limited changes, scheduled for completion by 31 December 2009. It is proposed that IPSAS ED 37 replace IPSAS 15 (cf. ED 37.62).

After its Meeting in Washington (May 2009), the IPSASB reaffirmed that it will continue its full consultation on IPSAS ED 37, ED 38 and ED 39, while recognizing the intention of the IASB to modify aspects of its current standards relating to the measurement of financial instruments due to the financial crisis. The IPSASB announced that it will consider any changes ultimately adopted by the IASB in due course.

IPSAS 16: Investment Property

Objective

The objective of IPSAS 16 is to prescribe the accounting treatment for investment property and related disclosure requirements.

The IFRS on which the IPSAS is based

IAS 40 "Investment Property"

Content

Principal definitions

Investment property is property (land or a building – or part of a building – or both) held to earn rentals or for capital appreciation or both, rather than for:

- Use in the production or supply of goods or services or for administrative purposes
- Sale in the ordinary course of operations

General remarks

Investment property generates cash flows largely independently of the other assets held by an entity, distinguishing it from other land or buildings controlled by public sector entities.

There are a number of circumstances in which public sector entities may hold property to earn rental and for capital appreciation. For example, a public sector entity (other than a GBE) may be established to manage a government's property portfolio on a commercial basis.

Scope

IPSAS 16 does not apply to owner-occupied property, property that is being constructed or developed for future use as investment property, and property held for sale in the ordinary course of operations.

Recognition

According to IPSAS 16.20, investment property should be recognized as an asset when, and only when:

    (a) It is probable that the future economic benefits of service potential that are associated with the investment property will flow to the entity.

(b) The cost or fair value of the investment property can be measured reliably.

Measurement of investment property: Initial measurement

According to IPSAS 16.23, an entity evaluates all its investment property costs at the time they are incurred. These costs include costs incurred initially to acquire an investment property and costs incurred subsequently to add to, replace part of, or service a property. However, the carrying amount of an investment property does not include the costs of the day-to-day servicing of such a property (cf. IPSAS 16.24). Rather, these costs are recognized in surplus or deficit as incurred. Costs of day-to-day servicing are primarily the costs of labor and consumables, and may include the cost of minor parts.

An investment property is measured initially at its cost. Transaction costs are included in the initial measurement. Where an investment property is acquired through a non-exchange transaction, its cost is measured at its fair value as at the date of acquisition.

Measurement of investment property after recognition

For the purpose of measurement after recognition, an entity can choose either the fair value model or the cost model:

- Fair value model: Investment property is measured at fair value. A gain or loss arising from a change in the fair value of investment property is recognized in surplus or deficit for the period in which it arises.
- Cost model: Investment property is measured at cost less any accumulated depreciation and any accumulated impairment losses (cf. IPSAS 17 "Property, Plant and Equipment").

The measurement model chosen must be applied uniformly to all investment property of the entity.

There is a rebuttable presumption that an entity can reliably determine the fair value of an investment property on a continuing basis. If an entity uses the fair value model and if there is clear evidence when the entity first acquires an item of investment property that the fair value of the investment property is not reliably determinable on a continuing basis, the entity must measure this investment property using the cost model in the subsequent periods until disposal. The residual value of this investment property is assumed to be zero.

Accounting treatment on disposal or retirement of investment property

An investment property should be derecognized (eliminated from the statement of financial position) on disposal or when the investment property is permanently withdrawn from use and no future economic benefits or service potential are expected from its disposal.

Gains or losses arising from the retirement or disposal of investment property are generally determined as the difference between the net disposal proceeds and the carrying amount of the asset and recognized in surplus or deficit in the period of the retirement or disposal.

Effective date

Periods beginning on or after 1 January 2008.

IPSAS 17: Property, Plant and Equipment

Objective

The objective of IPSAS 17 is to prescribe the accounting treatment for property, plant and equipment so that users of financial statements can discern information about an entity's investment in its property, plant and equipment and any changes in such investment. The principal issues in accounting for property, plant and equipment are the recognition of the assets, the determination of their carrying amounts and the depreciation charges and impairment losses to be recognized in relation to them.

The IFRS on which the IPSAS is based

IAS 16 "Property, Plant and Equipment"

Content

Principal definitions

Property, plant and equipment are tangible items that (a) are held for use in the production or supply of goods or services, for rental to others, or for administrative purposes; and (b) are expected to be used during more than one reporting period.

Recognition

According to IPSAS 17.14, the cost of an item of **property, plant and equipment** is recognized as an asset if, and only if:

(a) It is probable that the future economic benefits or service potential associated with the item will flow to the entity.

(b) The cost or fair value of the item can be measured reliably.

IPSAS 17 does not prescribe the unit of measure for recognition, i.e., what constitutes **an item of** property, plant and equipment. Thus, judgment is required in applying the recognition criteria to an entity's specific circumstances. It may be appropriate to aggregate individually insignificant items, such as library books and computer peripherals, and to apply the criteria to the aggregate value.

IPSAS 17 neither requires nor prohibits the recognition of heritage assets. An entity that recognizes heritage assets in its financial statements must apply the disclosure requirements of IPSAS 17 to the heritage assets recognized. However, it is not required to apply the other requirements of IPSAS 17 with respect to these heritage assets. However, acknowledging the significance and the problems related to recognizing and measuring heritage assets, the IPSASB developed a corresponding approach in the consultation paper "Accounting for Heritage Assets under the Accrual Basis of Accounting" in February 2006. The consultation paper is based on a joint initiative by the IPSASB with the UK standard setter (United Kingdom Accounting Standards Board (UK ASB)), which actually prepared the paper. The IPSASB has now analyzed the feedback on this consultation paper and is currently examining some further related points. A project brief is soon to be published on this basis.

Specialist military equipment will normally meet the definition of property, plant and equipment and must therefore be recognized as an asset. Infrastructure assets such as road networks or sewer systems must also be recognized in accordance with the principles of IPSAS 17.

Measurement of property, plant and equipment at recognition

An item of property, plant and equipment that qualifies for recognition as an asset should **initially be measured at its cost**.

IPSAS 17.30 provides that the cost of an item of property, plant and equipment comprises:

(a) Its purchase price, including import duties and non-refundable purchase taxes, after deducting trade discounts and rebates

(b) Any costs directly attributable to bringing the asset to the location and condition necessary for it to be capable of operating in the manner intended by management

(c) The initial estimate of the costs of dismantling and removing the item and restoring the site on which it is located, the obligation for which an entity incurs either when the item is acquired or as a consequence of having used the item during a particular period for purposes other than to produce inventories during that period

If an asset is acquired in a non-exchange transaction, its cost is determined at **fair value** at the time of acquisition. Items of property, plant and equipment acquired in an **exchange transaction** (including an exchange of similar items) are measured at fair value unless the exchange transaction lacks commercial substance or the fair value of neither the asset received nor the asset given up is reliably measurable (cf. IPSAS 17.38).

Measurement of property, plant and equipment after recognition

For the purpose of **measurement after recognition**, IPSAS 17.42 et seq. provides for a choice of two accounting models that must be applied uniformly to the entire class of property, plant and equipment:

- **Cost model**: The asset is carried at its cost less any accumulated depreciation and any accumulated impairment losses.
- **Revaluation model**: Subsequent to initial recognition as an asset, an item of property, plant and equipment whose fair value can be measured reliably should be carried at a revalued amount, being its fair value at the date of the revaluation less any subsequent accumulated depreciation and subsequent accumulated impairment losses.

A class of property, plant and equipment means a grouping of assets of a similar nature or function in an entity's operations. IPSAS 17.52 lists the following as examples of classes of property, plant and equipment: land, operational buildings, roads, machinery, aircraft, specialist military equipment, motor vehicles, etc.

If the revaluation model is used, revaluations should be made with sufficient regularity to ensure that the carrying amount does not differ materially from that which would be determined using fair value at the reporting date. Not just individual assets but all items of an existing class of property, plant and equipment must be remeasured in this case.

Accounting treatment for measurement of property, plant and equipment after recognition

If the carrying amount of a class of assets is increased as a result of a revaluation, the increase is credited directly to revaluation surplus. However, the increase is recognized in surplus or deficit to the extent that it reverses a revaluation decrease of the same class of assets previously recognized in surplus or deficit. If the carrying amount of a class of assets is decreased as a result of a revaluation, the decrease is initially debited directly to revaluation surplus relating to the same class of assets. To the extent that the decrease exceeds the amount of the corresponding revaluation surplus, the excess is recognized in surplus or deficit. If a remeasured asset is sold, the revaluation reserve is reclassified directly to revenue reserves. Recognition in surplus or deficit is not permissible.

Revaluation increases and decreases relating to individual assets within a class of property, plant and equipment must be offset against one another within that class. However, they must not be offset in respect of assets in different classes.

Each part of an item of property, plant and equipment with a cost that is significant in relation to the total cost of the item must be depreciated separately. In the case of a road system, for example, the formation, bridges, tunnels, lighting and footpaths must be depreciated separately.

Depreciation and impairment

Depreciation is charged systematically over the useful life. The depreciation charge for each period is recognized in surplus or deficit unless it is included in the carrying amount of another asset. The depreciation method must reflect the pattern in which the asset's future economic benefits or service potential is expected to be consumed by the entity. The residual value of an asset must be reviewed at least at each annual reporting date and must correspond to the amount that the entity would currently obtain from the disposal of the asset if the asset were already of the age and in the condition expected at the end of its useful life. If a condition of continuing to operate an item of property, plant and equipment (for example, an aircraft) is performing regular major inspections, the cost of each major inspection is recognized in the carrying amount of the item of property, plant and equipment as a replacement if the recognition criteria are satisfied. If expectations differ from previous estimates, the change(s) must be accounted for as a change in an accounting estimate in accordance with IPSAS 3, "Accounting Policies, Changes in Accounting Estimates and Errors."

Land and buildings are separable assets and are accounted for separately, even when they are acquired together. With some exceptions, such as quarries and sites used for landfill, land has an unlimited useful life and therefore is not depreciated. Buildings have a limited useful life and therefore are depreciable assets. An increase in the value of the land on which a building stands does not affect the determination of the depreciable amount of the building.

To determine whether an item of property, plant and equipment is **impaired**, an entity applies IPSAS 21, "Impairment of Non-Cash-Generating Assets" or IPSAS 26, "Impairment of Cash-Generating Assets".

Derecognition of property, plant and equipment

IPSAS 17.82 states that the carrying amount of an item of property, plant and equipment is derecognized:

*   On disposal

- When no future economic benefits or service potential is expected from its use or disposal

The gain or loss arising from the derecognition of an item of property, plant and equipment is included in surplus or deficit when the item is derecognized. Gains are not classified as revenue. The gain or loss arising from the derecognition of an item of property, plant and equipment is determined as the difference between the net disposal proceeds, if any, and the carrying amount of the item, regardless of whether it was previously measured at cost or fair value.

Extensive disclosures must be made for property, plant and equipment (cf. IPSAS 17.88 et seq.).

Effective date

Periods beginning on or after 1 January 2008.

IPSAS 18: Segment Reporting

Objective

The objective of IPSAS 18 is to establish principles for reporting financial information by segments. The disclosure of this information will:

(a) Help users of the financial statements to better understand the entity's past performance and to identify the resources allocated to support the major activities of the entity

(b) Enhance the transparency of financial reporting and enable the entity to better discharge its accountability obligations

The IFRS on which the IPSAS is based

IAS 14 "Segment Reporting" (as revised 1997)

Content

Principal definitions

A **segment** is a distinguishable activity or group of activities of an entity for which it is appropriate to separately report financial information for the purpose of evaluating the entity's past performance in achieving its objectives and for making decisions about the future allocation of resources.

IPSAS 18 distinguishes between **service segments** and **geographical segments.** A service segment refers to a distinguishable component of an entity that is engaged in providing related outputs or achieving particular operating objectives consistent with the overall mission of each entity. A geographical segment is a distinguishable component of an entity that is engaged in providing outputs or achieving particular operating objectives within a particular geographical area.

Scope

An entity which prepares and presents financial statements under the accrual basis of accounting should apply IPSAS 18 in the presentation of segment information. IPSAS 18 should be applied in complete sets of published financial statements that comply with International Public Sector Accounting Standards (cf. IPSAS 18.4).

If both consolidated financial statements of a government or other economic entity and the separate financial statements of the parent entity are presented together, segment information need be presented only on the basis of the consolidated financial statements.

Identification of reportable segments

An entity generally identifies service and geographical segments on the basis of its organizational structure and internal reporting system. In most cases, the major classifications of activities identified in budget documentation will best reflect the segment structure (cf. IPSAS 18.14). In most cases, the segments reported to the governing body and senior management of the public entity will also reflect the segments reported in the financial statements.

Government departments and agencies are usually managed along service lines because this reflects the way in which major outputs are identified. IPSAS 18.19 and IPSAS 18.22 set out criteria for defining service and geographical segments. Factors that will be considered in **determining** whether outputs (goods and services) are related and should be grouped as **segments** for financial reporting purposes according to IPSAS 18.19 include:

(a) The primary operating objectives of the entity and the goods, services and activities that relate to the achievement of each of those objectives and whether resources are allocated and budgeted on the basis of groups of goods and services

(b) The nature of the goods or services provided or activities undertaken

(c) The nature of the production process and/or service delivery and distribution process or mechanism

(d) The type of customer or consumer for the goods or services

(e) The way in which the entity is managed and financial information is reported to senior management and the governing board

(f) If applicable, the nature of the regulatory environment, (for example, department or statutory authority) or sectors of government (for example finance sector, public utilities, or general government)

The following factors are considered in **determining** whether financial information should be reported on a **geographical basis** (cf. IPSAS 18.22):

(a) Similarity of economic, social and political conditions in different regions

(b) Relationships between the primary objectives of the entity and the different regions

(c) Whether service delivery characteristics and operating conditions differ in different regions

(d) Whether this reflects the way in which the entity is managed and financial information is reported to senior management and the governing board

(e) Special needs, skills or risks associated with operations in a particular area

Segment disclosures

An entity must disclose **segment revenue** and **segment expense** for each segment (cf. IPSAS 18.27 for a definition of segment revenue and segment expense). Segment revenue from budget appropriation or similar allocation, segment revenue from other external sources, and segment revenue from transactions with other segments should be reported separately. An entity must also disclose the total carrying amount of **segment assets** and **segment liabilities** for each segment (cf. IPSAS 18.27 for a definition of segment assets and segment liabilities). An entity must further disclose the total cost incurred during the period to acquire segment assets that are expected to be used during more than one period for each segment (cf. IPSAS 18.52-56).

According to IPSAS 18.43, segment information should be prepared in conformity with the accounting policies adopted for preparing and presenting the financial statements of the consolidated group or entity.

IPSAS 18.47 states that assets that are jointly used by two or more segments should be allocated to segments if, and only if, their related revenues and expenses also are allocated to those segments.

If a segment is identified as a segment for the first time in the current period, prior period segment data that is presented for comparative purposes should be restated to reflect the newly reported segment as a separate segment, unless it is impracticable to do so (cf. IPSAS 18.49).

Multiple segmentation

Pursuant to IPSAS 18.23, an entity may report on the basis of more than one segment structure, for example by both service and geographical segments. A primary and secondary segment reporting structure can be adopted, with only limited disclosures made about secondary segments.

Disclosures

The disclosure requirements in IPSAS 18.52-75 must be made for each segment (cf. IPSAS 18.51).

Effective date

Periods beginning on or after 1 July 2003.

IPSAS 19: Provisions, Contingent Liabilities and Contingent Assets

Objective

The objective of IPSAS 19 is to define provisions, contingent liabilities and contingent assets, identify the circumstances in which provisions should be recognized, how they should be measured and the disclosures that should be made about them. The standard also requires that certain information be disclosed about contingent liabilities and contingent assets in the notes to the financial statements to enable users to understand their nature, timing and amount.

The IFRS on which the IPSAS is based

IAS 37 "Provisions, Contingent Liabilities and Contingent Assets"

Content

Principal definitions

A **liability** is a present obligation of the entity arising from past events, the settlement of which is expected to result in an outflow from the entity of resources embodying economic benefits or service potential.

A **provision** is a liability of uncertain timing or amount.

IPSAS 19.18 defines a **contingent liability** as:

(a) A possible obligation that arises from past events and whose existence will be confirmed only by the occurrence or non-occurrence of one or more uncertain future events not wholly within the control of the entity, or

(b) A present obligation that arises from past events but is not recognized because:

(i) It is not probable that an outflow of resources embodying economic benefits or service potential will be required to settle the obligation, or

(ii) The amount of the obligation cannot be measured with sufficient reliability.

IPSAS 19.18 defines a **contingent asset** as a possible asset that arises from past events and whose existence will be confirmed only by the occurrence or

114

non-occurrence of one or more uncertain future events not wholly within the control of the entity.

Scope

IPSAS 19.1 expressly states that accounting for provisions and contingent liabilities arising from **social benefits** provided by an entity for which it does not receive consideration that is approximately equal to the value of goods and services provided directly in return from the recipients of those benefits is not regulated by IPSAS 19. Also, IPSAS 19 does not apply to **financial instruments** that are carried at fair value.

Recognition

According to IPSAS 19.22 a **provision** should be recognized when

(a) An entity has a present obligation (legal or constructive) as a result of a past event,

(b) It is probable that an outflow of resources embodying economic benefits or service potential will be required to settle the obligation, and

(c) A reliable estimate can be made of the amount of the obligation.

If these conditions are not met, no provision should be recognized.

It may not always be clear whether there is a present obligation. In these cases, a past event is deemed to give rise to a present obligation if, taking account of all available evidence, it is more likely than not that a present obligation exists at the reporting date. IPSAS 19.24 gives a lawsuit as an example.

IPSAS 19.35 and 19.39 provide that an entity should not recognize contingent liabilities or contingent assets.

Measurement

The amount recognized as a provision should be the best estimate of the expenditure required to settle the present obligation at the reporting date. According to IPSAS 19.45, the best estimate of the expenditure required to settle the present obligation is the amount that an entity would rationally pay to settle the obligation at the reporting date or to transfer it to a third party at that time. The estimates of outcome and financial effect are determined mainly by the judgment of the management of the entity (cf. IPSAS 19.46). Additional, objective sources of information therefore include experience of similar transactions and, in some cases, reports from independent experts.

Events after the reporting date must also be taken into account in the estimates (cf. IPSAS 19.46).

To determine the best estimate, IPSAS 19.47 et seq. refers − by analogy to IAS 37.39 et seq. − to a statistical method of estimation which corresponds to the **expected value** under IPSAS 19.47. According to IPSAS 19.47, the expected value method should be used when the provision being measured involves a large population of items and the obligation is based on a distribution of probabilities. The overall scope of obligations is estimated by weighting all possible outcomes by their associated probabilities. Where there is a continuous range of possible outcomes, and each point in that range is as likely as any other, the mid-point of the range is used.

Where a single obligation is being measured and no statistical experience is available, IPSAS 19.48 provides that the individual most likely outcome may be the best estimate of the liability. According to IPSAS 19.50, the risks and uncertainties that inevitably surround many events and circumstances should be taken into account in reaching the best estimate of a provision. This means that other possible developments must also be included that can necessitate a higher or lower provision depending on the circumstances. However, IPSAS 19.51 does not encourage overcautious accounting.

Where the effect of the time value of money is material, the amount of a provision should be the present value of the expenditures expected to be required to settle the obligation (cf. IPSAS 19.53). This should serve to avoid overstatement of provisions. For this reason, future outflows of resources expected must be discounted.

Future events that may affect the amount required to settle an obligation should be reflected in the amount of a provision where there is sufficient objective evidence that they will occur (cf. IPSAS 19.58). If future events relate to possible new legislation, its effects can only be taken into account by the public sector entity when it is virtually certain to be enacted (cf. IPSAS 19.60).

Reimbursements

Where some or all of the expenditure required to settle a provision is expected to be reimbursed by another party, the reimbursement should be recognized when, and only when, it is virtually certain that reimbursement will be received if the entity settles the obligation. The reimbursement should be treated as a separate asset. The amount recognized for the reimbursement should not exceed the amount of the provision. In the statement of financial performance, the expense relating to a provision may be presented net of the amount recognized for a reimbursement.

Changes in and use of provisions

Provisions should be reviewed at each reporting date and adjusted to reflect the current best estimate. If it is no longer probable that an outflow of resources embodying economic benefits or service potential will be required to settle the obligation, the provision should be reversed (cf. IPSAS 19.69).

A provision should be used only for expenditures for which the provision was originally recognized (cf. IPSAS 19.71).

Application of the recognition and measurement rules

Provisions should not be recognized for net deficits from future operating activities (cf. IPSAS 19.73). If an entity has a contract that is onerous, the present obligation (net of recoveries) under the contract should be recognized and measured as a provision (cf. IPSAS 19.76).

IPSAS 19.81 et seq. discusses the recognition and measurement of provisions for restructuring measures.

Disclosures in the notes

For each class of provision, an entity should disclose (cf. IPSAS 19.97):

    (a)   The carrying amount at the beginning and end of the period

    (b)   Additional provisions made in the period, including increases in existing provisions

    (c)   Amounts used (i.e., incurred and charged against the provision) during the period

    (d)   Unused amounts reversed during the period

    (e)   The increase during the period in the discounted amount arising from the passage of time and the effect of any change in the discount rate

Comparative information is not required.

An entity should disclose the following for each class of provision (cf. IPSAS 19.98):

    (a)   A brief description of the nature of the obligation and the expected timing of any resulting outflows of economic benefits or service potential

(b) An indication of the uncertainties about the amount or timing of those outflows. Where necessary to provide adequate information, an entity should disclose the major assumptions made concerning future events, as addressed in IPSAS 19.58

(c) The amount of any expected reimbursement, stating the amount of any asset that has been recognized for that expected reimbursement

Further disclosure requirements in relation to provisions, contingent liabilities and contingent assts can be found in IPSAS 19.99 et seq.

Effective date

Periods beginning on or after 1 January 2004.

IPSAS 20: Related Party Disclosures

Objective

The objective of IPSAS 20 is to require the disclosure of the existence of related party relationships where control exists. The disclosure of information about transactions between the entity and its related parties is also required in certain circumstances. This information is required for accountability purposes and to facilitate a better understanding of the financial position and performance of the reporting entity. The principal issues in disclosing information about related parties are identifying which parties control or significantly influence the reporting entity and determining what information should be disclosed about transactions with those parties.

The IFRS on which the IPSAS is based

IAS 24 "Related Party Disclosures"

Content

Principal definitions

Related party: Parties are considered to be **related** if one party has the ability to control the other party or exercise significant influence over the other party in making financial and operating decisions or if the related party entity and another entity are subject to common control. Related parties include entities that directly, or indirectly through one or more intermediaries, control, or are controlled by the reporting entity; associates; individuals owning, directly or indirectly, an interest in the reporting entity that gives them significant influence over the entity, and close members of the family of any such individual; key management personnel, and close members of the family of key management personnel.

Key management personnel are all directors or members of the governing body of the entity, where that body has the authority and responsibility for planning, directing and controlling the activities of the entity (cf. IPSAS 20.6). At the whole-of-government level, the governing body may consist of elected or appointed representatives (for example, a president or governor, ministers, councilors and aldermen or their nominees).

Disclosure requirements

According to IPSAS 20.25, related party relationships where control exists should be disclosed irrespective of whether there have been transactions between the related parties.

In respect of transactions between related parties other than transactions that would occur within a normal supplier or client/recipient relationship on terms and conditions no more or less favorable than those which it is reasonable to expect the entity would have adopted if dealing with that individual or entity at arm's length in the same circumstances, the reporting entity should disclose (cf. IPSAS 20.27):

(a) The nature of the related party relationships

(b) The types of transactions that have occurred

(c) The elements of the transactions necessary to clarify the significance of these transactions to its operations and sufficient to enable the financial statements to provide relevant and reliable information for decision making and accountability purposes

The following are examples of situations where related party transactions may lead to disclosures by a reporting entity (cf. IPSAS 20.28):

(a) Rendering or receiving of services

(b) Purchases or transfers/sales of goods (finished or unfinished)

(c) Purchases or transfers/sales of property and other assets

(d) Agency arrangements

(e) Leasing arrangements

(f) Transfer of research and development

(g) License agreements

(h) Finance (including loans and capital contributions)

(i) Guarantees and collateral

According to IPSAS 20.32, items of a similar nature may be disclosed in aggregate except when separate disclosure is necessary to provide relevant and reliable information for decision making and accountability purposes.

An entity must disclose the following in relation to the **remuneration of key management personnel** (cf. IPSAS 20.34):

(a) The aggregate remuneration of key management personnel and the number of individuals, determined on a full time equivalent basis, receiving remuneration within this category. This must show separately major classes of key management personnel, including a description of each class.

(b) The total amount of all other remuneration and compensation provided to key management personnel, and close members of the family of key management personnel, by the reporting entity during the reporting period showing separately the aggregate amounts provided to:

(i) Key management personnel

(ii) Close members of the family of key management personnel.

(c) In respect of loans which are not widely available to persons who are not key management personnel and loans whose availability is not widely known by members of the public, for each individual member of key management personnel and each close member of the family of key management personnel:

(i) The amount of loans advanced during the period and terms and conditions thereof

(ii) The amount of loans repaid during the period

(iii) The amount of the closing balance of all loans and receivables

(iv) Provided the individual is not a director or member of the governing body or senior management group of the entity, the relationship of the individual to such.

Structure of disclosures pursuant to IPSAS 20

The appendix to IPSAS 20 contains examples of how disclosures on related parties can be structured.

Effective date

Periods beginning on or after 1 January 2004.

IPSAS 21: Impairment of Non-Cash-Generating Assets

Objective

The objective of IPSAS 21 is to prescribe the procedures that an entity applies to determine whether a non-cash-generating asset is impaired and to ensure that impairment losses are recognized. The standard also specifies when an entity would reverse an impairment loss and prescribes disclosures.

The IFRS on which the IPSAS is based

IAS 36 "Impairment of Assets" generally corresponds to IPSAS 21. However, as IPSAS 21 relates solely to non-cash-generating assets, IAS 36 and IPSAS 21 do not correspond in all respects.

Content

Principal definitions

Cash-generating assets are assets held with the primary objective of generating a commercial return. **Non-cash-generating assets** are assets not held with the primary objective of generating a commercial return (cf. IPSAS 21.14).

Depreciation (amortization) is the systematic allocation of the depreciable amount of an asset over its useful life.

IPSAS 21.14 states that impairment is a loss in the future economic benefits or service potential of an asset, over and above the systematic recognition of the loss of the asset's future economic benefits or service potential through depreciation.

Recoverable service amount is the higher of a non-cash-generating asset's fair value less costs to sell and its value in use. **Value in use** of a non-cash-generating asset is the present value of the asset's remaining service potential.

An **impairment loss** of a non-cash-generating asset is the amount by which the carrying amount of an asset exceeds its recoverable amount.

Scope

IPSAS 21 generally applies to all non-cash-generating assets.

IPSAS 21 does not apply to:

(a) Inventories (cf. IPSAS 12 "Inventories")

(b) Assets arising from construction contracts (cf. IPSAS 11 "Construction Contracts")

(c) Financial assets that are included in the scope of IPSAS 15 "Financial Instruments: Disclosure and Presentation"

(d) Investment property that is measured using the fair value model (cf. IPSAS 16 "Investment Property")

(e) Non-cash-generating property, plant and equipment that is measured at revalued amounts (cf. IPSAS 17 "Property, Plant and Equipment")

(f) Other assets in respect of which accounting requirements for impairment are included in another IPSAS

Public sector entities that hold cash-generating assets must apply IPSAS 26 "Impairment of Cash-Generating Assets" to such assets.

Measurement procedure

A **non-cash-generating asset** is **impaired** when the carrying amount of the asset exceeds its recoverable service amount. The **recoverable service amount** is the higher of the non-cash-generating asset's fair value less costs to sell and its value in use.

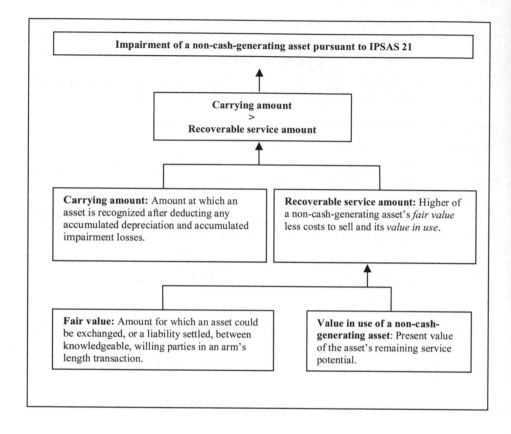

Figure 5: Impairment of a non-cash-generating assets

Impairment testing

IPSAS 21.26 states that an entity must assess at each reporting date whether there is any indication that an asset may be impaired. If any such indication exists, the entity must estimate the recoverable service amount of the asset.

IPSAS 21.27 describes some indications that show whether an asset is impaired. A distinction is made between internal and external sources of information. If any one of those indications is present, an entity is required to make a formal estimate of the recoverable service amount. If no indication of a potential impairment loss is present, IPSAS 21 does not require an entity to make a formal estimate of recoverable service amount.

It is not always necessary to determine both an asset's fair value less costs to sell and its value in use. If either of these amounts exceeds the asset's carrying amount, the asset is not impaired and it is not necessary to estimate the other amount.

Measuring recoverable service amount

a) Determining fair value less costs to sell

It may be possible to determine fair value less costs to sell, even if an asset is not traded in an active market. If there is no active market for an asset, IPSAS 21.42 describes possible alternative approaches to determine the fair value less costs to sell. However, sometimes it will not be possible to determine fair value less costs to sell because there is no basis for making a reliable estimate of the amount obtainable from the sale of the asset in an arm's length transaction between knowledgeable and willing parties. In this case the entity can use the value in use of the asset as its recoverable service amount.

b) Determining value in use

Unlike IAS 36, IPSAS 21 defines the **value in use of a non-cash-generating asset** as the present value of the asset's remaining service potential. The present value of the remaining service potential of a non-cash-generating asset is determined using one of following three approaches, depending on the data available and the nature of the impairment (cf. IPSAS 21.45-49).

- **Depreciated replacement cost approach** (cf. IPSAS 21.45 et seq.): The present value of the remaining service potential of an asset is determined as the depreciated replacement cost of the asset. The replacement cost of an asset is the cost to replace the asset's gross service potential. This cost of the asset is depreciated to adequately reflect the technical, physical and/or economic ageing of the asset. An asset may be replaced either through reproduction (replication) of the existing asset or through replacement of its gross service potential. The depreciated replacement cost is measured as the reproduction or replacement cost of the asset, whichever is lower, less accumulated depreciation calculated on the basis of such cost, to reflect the already consumed or expired service potential of the asset.
- **Restoration cost approach** (cf. IPSAS 21.48): The present value of the remaining service potential of the asset is determined by subtracting the estimated restoration cost of the asset from the current cost of replacing the remaining service potential of the asset before impairment. The latter cost is usually determined as the depreciated reproduction or replacement cost of the asset, whichever is lower.

- **Service units approach** (cf. IPSAS 21.49): The present value of the remaining service potential of the asset is determined by reducing the current cost of the remaining service potential of the asset before impairment to conform to the reduced number of service units expected from the asset in its impaired state. As in the restoration cost approach, the current cost of replacing the remaining service potential of the asset before impairment is usually determined as the depreciated reproduction or replacement cost of the asset before impairment, whichever is lower.

The choice of the most appropriate approach to measuring value in use depends on the availability of data and the nature of the impairment (cf. IPSAS 21.50 for more detail). The figure below gives an overview of the choice of the most appropriate approach for determining the value in use of a non-cash-generating asset:

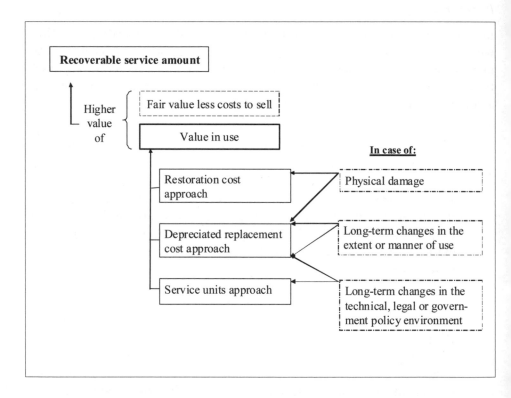

Figure 6: Determination of the recoverable service amount

Recognition and measurement of an impairment loss

According to IPSAS 21.52, if, and only if, the recoverable amount of an asset is less than its carrying amount, the carrying amount of the asset must be reduced to its recoverable service amount. That reduction is an **impairment loss**.

IPSAS 21.54 states that an impairment loss must be recognized immediately in surplus or deficit. When the amount estimated for an impairment loss is greater than the carrying amount of the asset to which it relates, an entity must recognize a liability if, and only if, that is required by another IPSAS (IPSAS 21.55).

After the recognition of an impairment loss, the depreciation (amortization) charge for the asset must be adjusted in future periods to allocate the asset's revised carrying amount, less its residual value (if any), on a systematic basis over its remaining useful life (cf. IPSAS 21.57).

Reversing an impairment loss

In relation to potential reversals, an entity should assess at each reporting date whether there is any indication that an impairment loss recognized for an asset in prior periods may no longer exist or may have decreased (cf. IPSAS 21.59). If any such indication exists, the entity must estimate the recoverable service amount of that asset. A reversal of an impairment loss recorded in prior years is permissible in certain circumstances. IPSAS 21.60 describes indications that an impairment loss recognized in prior periods for an asset may no longer exist or may have decreased. Again, a distinction is made between internal and external sources of information.

According to IPSAS 21.65, an impairment loss recognized in prior periods for an asset is reversed if, and only if, there has been a change in the estimates used to determine the asset's recoverable service amount since the last impairment loss was recognized. If this is the case, the carrying amount of the asset must, except as described in IPSAS 21.68, be increased to its recoverable amount. That increase is a reversal of an impairment loss.

The increased carrying amount of an asset attributable to a reversal of an impairment loss cannot exceed the carrying amount that would have been determined (net of depreciation or amortization) if no impairment loss had been recognized for the asset in prior periods (= amortized cost).

A reversal of an impairment loss for an asset is recognized immediately in surplus or deficit pursuant to IPSAS 21.69.

After a reversal of an impairment loss is recognized, the depreciation (amortization) charge for the asset must be adjusted in future periods to allocate the asset's revised carrying amount, less its residual value (if any), on a systematic basis over its remaining useful life.

Redesignation of cash-generating and non-cash-generating assets

The redesignation of assets from cash-generating assets to non-cash-generating assets or from non-cash-generating assets to cash-generating assets can only occur when there is clear evidence that such a redesignation is appropriate. A redesignation, by itself, does not necessarily trigger an impairment test or a reversal of an impairment loss. Instead, the indication for an impairment test or a reversal of an impairment loss arises from, as a minimum, the listed indications applicable to the asset after redesignation.

Disclosure requirements

An entity must disclose the criteria developed by the entity to distinguish cash-generating assets from non-cash-generating assets.

Further disclosure requirements in relation to non-cash-generating assets and non-cash-generating units can be found in IPSAS 21.73 et seq.

Effective date

Periods beginning on or after 1 January 2006.

IPSAS 22: Disclosure of Information About the General Government Sector

Objective

The objective of this standard is to prescribe disclosure requirements for governments which elect to present information about the **general government sector** (GGS) in their consolidated financial statements. The disclosure of appropriate information about the GGS can enhance the transparency of financial reports, and provide for a better understanding of the relationship between the market and non-market activities of the public sector and between financial statements and statistical bases of financial reporting.

The IFRS on which the IPSAS is based

IPSAS 22 is an IPSAS specifically for the public sector. As a result there is no IFRS equivalent.

Content

Principal definitions

Under statistical bases of financial reporting the **public sector** comprises the **general government sector** (GGS), the **public financial corporations sector** (PFCS) and **public non-financial corporations sector** (PNFCS). The general government sector encompasses the central operations of government and typically includes all those resident non-market non-profit entities that have their operations funded primarily by the government and government entities. The general government sector does not include public financial corporations or public non-financial corporations (cf. IPSAS 22.18). The public non-financial corporations sector includes for example publicly owned utilities.

Scope

IPSAS 22 only applies for governments that prepare and present consolidated financial statements under the accrual basis of accounting and elect to disclose financial information about the general government sector (cf. IPSAS 22.2).

Financial statements for the government and statistical bases of financial reporting

While financial statements consolidate only controlled entities, these provisions do not apply for statistical bases of financial reporting. The consolidated group in accounting therefore differs from that in the statistical bases of financial reporting. The **general government sector** according to the **System of National Accounts 93** (SNA 93) comprises all national, state/provincial and local government levels, social insurance at all administrative levels as well as non-profit entities which undertake non-market activities controlled by public entities in the country of residence. It usually includes public entities such as government agencies, courts, public educational institutions, public medical care providers and other official entities.

Accounting policies for the general government sector

According to IPSAS 22.23, financial information about the general government sector must be disclosed in conformity with the accounting policies adopted for preparing and presenting the consolidated financial statements of the government.

However, the general government sector does not apply the requirements of IPSAS 6 "Consolidated and Separate Financial Statements" in respect of entities in the public financial corporations and public non-financial corporations sectors. IPSAS 22 reflects the view that the consolidated financial statements of a government which elects to disclose information about the general government sector are to be disaggregated to present the general government sector as one sector of the government reporting entity (cf. IPSAS 22.26).

According to IPSAS 22.25, the general government sector must recognize its investment in the public financial corporations sector and public non-financial corporations sector as an asset and must account for that asset at the carrying amount of the net assets of its investees.

Disclosures in the notes

Disclosures made in respect of the general government sector must include at least the following:

    (a)   Assets by major class, showing separately the investment in other sectors

    (b)   Liabilities by major class

(c) Net assets/equity

(d) Total revaluation increments and decrements and other items of revenue and expense recognized directly in net assets/equity

(e) Revenue by major class

(f) Expenses by major class

(g) Surplus or deficit

(h) Cash flows from operating activities by major class

(i) Cash flows from investing activities

(j) Cash flows from financing activities

The manner of presentation of the general government sector disclosures should be no more prominent than the government's financial statements prepared in accordance with IPSASs (cf. IPSAS 22.35).

According to IPSAS 22.40, entities preparing general government sector disclosures must disclose the significant controlled entities that are included in the general government sector. IPSAS 22 also requires disclosures on changes in those entities from the prior period, together with an explanation of the reasons why any such entity that was previously included in the general government sector is no longer included.

According to IPSAS 22.43 the general government sector disclosures must be reconciled to the consolidated financial statements of the government showing separately the amount of the adjustment to each equivalent item in those financial statements.

Effective date

Periods beginning on or after 1 January 2008.

IPSAS 23: Revenue from Non-Exchange Transactions (Taxes and Transfers)

Objective

The objective of IPSAS 23 is to prescribe requirements for the financial reporting of revenue arising from non-exchange transactions, other than non-exchange transactions that give rise to an entity combination. The standard deals with issues that need to be considered in recognizing and measuring revenue from non-exchange transactions including the identification of contributions from owners. While the revenue of public sector entities stems both from exchange and non-exchange transactions, most transactions at public sector entities are non-exchange transactions. In particular, these include revenue from taxes and transfers (both cash and non-cash transfers).

The IFRS on which the IPSAS is based

IPSAS 23 is an IPSAS specifically for the public sector. As a result, there is no IFRS equivalent.

Content

Principal definitions

Exchange transactions are transactions in which one entity receives assets or services, or has liabilities extinguished, and directly gives approximately equal value (primarily in the form of cash, goods, services, or use of assets) to another entity in exchange.

Non-exchange transactions are transactions that are not exchange transactions. In a non-exchange transaction, an entity either receives value from another entity without directly giving approximately equal value in exchange, or gives value to another entity without directly receiving approximately equal value in exchange.

IPSAS 23 defines **taxes** as economic benefits or service potential compulsorily paid or payable to public sector entities, in accordance with laws and/or regulations, established to provide revenue to the government. Taxes do not include fines or other penalties imposed for breaches of the law.

Fines are economic benefits or service potential received or receivable by public sector entities, as determined by a court or other law enforcement body, as a consequence of the breach of laws or regulations.

Transfers are inflows of future economic benefits or service potential from non-exchange transactions, other than taxes.

Stipulations on transferred assets are terms in laws or regulation, or a binding arrangement, imposed upon the use of a transferred asset by entities external to the reporting entity.

Conditions on transferred assets are stipulations that specify that the future economic benefits or service potential embodied in the asset is required to be consumed by the recipient as specified or future economic benefits or service potential must be returned to the transferor.

Restrictions on transferred assets are stipulations that limit or direct the purposes for which a transferred asset may be used, but do not specify that future economic benefits or service potential is required to be returned to the transferor if not deployed as specified.

A **present obligation** is a duty to act or perform in a certain way and may give rise to a liability in respect of any non-exchange transaction (cf. IPSAS 23.51). Present obligations may be imposed by stipulations in laws or regulations or binding arrangements establishing the basis of transfers. They may also arise from the normal operating environment, such as the recognition of advance receipts.

Recognition and measurement of assets from non-exchange transactions

Under IPSAS 23.31, an inflow of resources from a non-exchange transaction, other than services in-kind, that meets the definition of an asset is recognized as an asset when, and only when:

(a) It is probable that the future economic benefits or service potential associated with the asset will flow to the entity, and

(b) The fair value of the asset can be measured reliably.

An inflow of resources from a non-exchange transaction is probable when the inflow is more likely than not to occur (cf. IPSAS 23.35).

According to IPSAS 23.42, an asset acquired through a non-exchange transaction is initially measured at its **fair value** as at the date of acquisition.

Recognition of revenue from non-exchange transactions

IPSAS 23.44 states that an inflow of resources from a non-exchange transaction recognized as an asset is recognized as **revenue**, except to the extent that a liability is also recognized in respect of the same inflow. This is generally the case if and for as long as the future inflow of resources is contingent on unsatisfied conditions.

When an entity satisfies a present obligation recognized as a liability in respect of an inflow of resources from a non-exchange transaction recognized as an asset, it reduces the carrying amount of the liability recognized and recognizes an amount of revenue equal to that reduction.

Measurement of revenue from non-exchange transactions

Revenue from non-exchange transactions is measured at the amount of the increase in net assets recognized by the entity.

Present obligations recognized as liabilities

According to IPSAS 23.50, a **present obligation** arising from a non-exchange transaction that meets the definition of a liability is recognized as a liability when, and only when:

(a) It is probable that an outflow of resources embodying future economic benefits or service potential will be required to settle the obligation, and

(b) A reliable estimate can be made of the amount of the obligation.

According to IPSAS 23.51, a present obligation is a duty to act or perform in a certain way and may give rise to a liability in respect of any non-exchange transaction. Present obligations may be imposed by stipulations in laws or regulations or binding arrangements establishing the basis of transfers. They may also arise from the normal operating environment, such as the recognition of advance receipts.

In many instances, taxes are levied and assets are transferred to public sector entities in non-exchange transactions pursuant to laws, regulations or other binding arrangements that impose stipulations that they be used for particular purposes. In turn, the statutory regulations provide that these assets can only be used for certain purposes. For example, these can include taxes, the use of which is limited by laws or other legal regulations to specified purposes, or transfers, established by a binding arrangement that includes conditions.

Conditions on a transferred asset thus give rise to a present obligation on initial recognition that will be recognized when the criteria for recognition as a liability are fulfilled (cf. IPSAS 23.55). The amount recognized as a liability is the best estimate of the amount required to settle the present obligation at the reporting date.

Accounting for taxes

An entity must recognize an asset in respect of **taxes** when the taxable event occurs and the asset recognition criteria are met (cf. IPSAS 23.59). The taxable event is determined by the government, parliament or another authorized body and the taxable event is the subject of taxation. In the case of income tax, for example, the taxable event is the taxable income of the taxpayer in a tax period.

According to IPSAS 23.71, taxation revenue is determined at a gross amount. It is not reduced for expenses paid through the tax system. It cannot be reduced by other types of expenses (e.g., subsidies to health insurance premiums) that are paid in a simplified manner through the tax system, for example by offsetting against the tax liability. In fact, the (collected) taxation revenue must be increased by expenses paid through the tax system for the presentation in the financial statements (cf. IPSAS 23.71).

IPSAS 23.73 states that taxation revenue cannot be grossed up for the amount of **tax expenditures**. In most jurisdictions, governments use the tax system to encourage certain financial behavior and discourage other behavior. For example, in some jurisdictions, home owners are permitted to deduct mortgage interest and property taxes from their gross income when calculating tax assessable income. These types of concessions are available only to taxpayers. If an entity (including a natural person) does not pay tax, it cannot make use of the concession. In the public sector, these types of concessions are called tax expenditures. Tax expenditures are foregone revenue, not expenses, and do not give rise to inflows or outflows of resources – that is, they do not give rise to assets, liabilities, revenue or expenses of the taxing government.

The key distinction between expenses paid through the tax system and tax expenditures is that for expenses paid through the tax system, the amount is available to recipients irrespective of whether they pay taxes, or use a particular mechanism to pay their taxes.

Accounting for transfers

An entity must recognize an asset in respect of **transfers** when the transferred resources meet the definition of an asset and satisfy the criteria for recognition as an asset (cf. IPSAS 23.76 et seq.). Transferred assets are also measured at fair value at the date of acquisition.

The following transfer revenue is accounted for as follows:

(1) Fines (IPSAS 23.88 et seq.)

Fees, fines and penalties as determined by a court or other law enforcement body give rise to receivables. They are recognized when the receivable meets the definition of an asset and fulfills the recognition criteria in IPSAS 23.31. They do not impose on the recipient any obligations which may be recognized as a liability. Assets arising from fines are measured at the best estimate of the inflow of resources to the entity.

(2) Bequests (IPSAS 23.90 et seq.)

A bequest is a transfer made according to the provisions of a deceased person's will. According to IPSAS 23.90, the past event giving rise to the control of resources embodying future economic benefits or service potential for a bequest occurs when the entity has an enforceable claim, for example on the death of the testator, or the granting of probate, depending on the laws of the jurisdiction. Bequests which satisfy the definition of an asset and meet the recognition criteria are recognized as assets. Determining the probability of an inflow of future economic benefits or service potential may be problematic if a period of time elapses between the death of the testator and the entity receiving any assets. Bequests are generally measured at fair value at the date of acquisition.

(3) Gifts and donations, including goods in-kind (IPSAS 23.93 et seq.)

Gifts and donations are voluntary transfers of assets including cash or other monetary assets, goods in-kind and services in-kind that one entity makes to another, normally free from stipulations. Cash or other monetary gifts or donations as well as goods in-kind are generally recognized on the date on which the gift or donation is received. The recognition criteria pursuant to IPSAS 23.31 apply. Services in-kind are subject to different provisions. Goods in-kind are generally recognized as assets upon receipt of the goods. If goods in-kind are received without conditions attached, revenue is recognized immediately. If conditions are attached, a liability is recognized, which is reduced and revenue recognized as the conditions are satisfied.

On initial recognition, gifts and donations including goods in-kind are measured at their fair value as at the date of acquisition, which may be ascertained by reference to an active market, or by appraisal. An appraisal of the value of an asset is normally undertaken by a member of the valuation profession who holds a recognized and relevant professional qualification.

(4) Services in-kind (IPSAS 23.98 et seq.)

Services in-kind provided by individuals to public sector entities in a non-exchange transaction can be recognized as an asset in surplus or deficit. The standard provides an option in this case.

Effective date

Periods beginning on or after 30 June 2008.

IPSAS 24: Presentation of Budget Information in Financial Statements

Objective

IPSAS 24 requires a comparison of budget amounts and the actual amounts arising from execution of the budget to be included in the financial statements of entities which are required to, or elect to, make publicly available their approved budget(s) and for which they are, therefore, held publicly accountable. The standard also requires disclosure of an explanation of the reasons for material differences between the budget and actual amounts. Compliance with the requirements of this standard will ensure that public sector entities discharge their accountability obligations and enhance the transparency of their financial statements by demonstrating compliance with the approved budget(s) for which they are held publicly accountable and, where the budget(s) and the financial statements are prepared on the same basis, their financial performance in achieving the budgeted results.

The IFRS on which the IPSAS is based

IPSAS 24 is an IPSAS specifically for the public sector. As a result there is no IFRS equivalent.

Content

Principal definitions

IPSAS 24 defines the **original budget** as the initial approved budget for the budget period.

Approved budget means the expenditure authority derived from laws, appropriation bills, government ordinances and other decisions related to the anticipated revenue or receipts for the budgetary period.

Final budget is the original budget adjusted for all reserves, carry over amounts, transfers, allocations, supplemental appropriations, and other authorized legislative, or similar authority, changes applicable to the budget period.

Scope

IPSAS 24 applies to public sector entities that are required or elect to make publicly available their approved budget(s).

Presentation of a comparison of budget and actual amounts

In accordance with IPSAS 24.14, an entity must present a comparison of the budget amounts for which it is held publicly accountable and actual amounts either as a separate additional financial statement (referred to as a statement of comparison of budget and actual amounts) or as additional budget columns in the financial statements currently presented in accordance with IPSASs.

The comparison of budget and actual amounts must present separately for each level of legislative oversight (cf. IPSAS 24.14):

(a)   The original and final budget amounts

(b)   The actual amounts on a comparable basis

(c)   By way of note disclosure, an explanation of material differences between the budget for which the entity is held publicly accountable and actual amounts, unless such explanation is included in other public documents issued in conjunction with the financial statements and a cross reference to those documents is made in the notes

In general IPSAS 24 provides that all comparisons of budget and actual amounts must be presented on a comparable basis to the budget (cf. IPSAS 24.31). According to IPSAS 24.21, an entity must present a comparison of budget and actual amounts as additional budget columns in the primary financial statements only where the financial statements and the budget are prepared on a comparable basis. For example, if the budget is prepared on the cash basis and the financial statements are prepared on the accrual basis, no comparison as additional budget columns is necessary. If the financial statements and the budget were prepared on a comparable basis, additional columns can be added to the existing primary financial statements presented in accordance with IPSASs. These additional columns will identify original and final budget amounts and, if the entity so chooses, differences between the budget and actual amounts.

When the budget and financial statements are not prepared on a comparable basis, IPSAS 24.23 provides for a separate **statement of comparison of budget and actual amounts**. In these cases, to ensure that readers do not misinterpret financial information which is prepared on different bases, the financial statements could usefully clarify that the budget and the accounting bases differ and the statement of comparison of budget and actual amounts is prepared on the budget basis.

Disclosure requirements

Pursuant to IPSAS 24.29, an entity must present an explanation of whether changes between the original and final budget are a consequence of reallocations within the budget, or of other factors. This can be disclosed in the notes to the financial statements or in a report issued before, at the same time as, or in conjunction with the financial statements. In the latter case, it must include a cross-reference to the report in the notes to the financial statements.

Note disclosures of budgetary basis, period and scope

An entity must explain in the notes to the financial statements the budgetary basis and classification basis adopted in the approved budget (cf. IPSAS 24.39). An entity must also disclose in the notes to the financial statements the period of the approved budget (cf. IPSAS 24.43) and the entities included in the approved budget (cf. IPSAS 24.45).

Reconciliation

Where the financial statements and budget are not prepared on a comparable basis, the actual amounts presented on a comparable basis to the budget must be reconciled to the amounts presented in the financial statements (cf. IPSAS 24.47). Differences must be explained. Reconciliation must be made for the following items:

    (a)   If the accrual basis is adopted for the budget, total revenues, total expenses and net cash flows from operating activities, investing activities and financing activities

    (b)   If a basis other than the accrual basis is adopted for the budget, net cash flows from operating activities, investing activities and financing activities

Differences can stem from the accounting basis, timing differences between the budget and the financial statements and entity differences in the consolidated group. The reconciliation must be presented either in the comparison of budget and actual amounts or in the notes to the financial statements.

Effective date

Periods beginning on or after 1 January 2009.

Objective

The objective of IPSAS 25 is to provide guidance for the accounting and disclosure of employee benefits. The standard requires an entity to recognize

(a) A liability when an employee has provided service in exchange for employee benefits to be paid in the future

(b) An expense when the entity consumes the economic benefits or service potential arising from service provided by an employee in exchange for employee benefits

The IFRS on which the IPSAS is based

IAS 19 "Employee Benefits"

Content

Principal definitions

Employee benefits are all forms of consideration given by an entity in exchange for service rendered by employees.

Short-term employee benefits are employee benefits (other than termination benefits and equity compensation benefits) which fall due wholly within 12 months after the end of the period in which the employees render the related service.

Postemployment benefits are employee benefits (other than termination benefits and equity compensation benefits) which are payable after the completion of employment.

Other long-term employee benefits are employee benefits (other than post-employment benefits and termination benefits) which do not fall due wholly within 12 months after the end of the period in which the employees render the related service.

Termination benefits are employee benefits payable as a result of either:

(a) An entity's decision to terminate an employee's employment before the normal retirement date, or

(b) An employee's decision to accept voluntary redundancy in exchange for those benefits.

Postemployment benefit plans are formal or informal arrangements under which an entity provides postemployment benefits for one or more employees.

Defined contribution plans are postemployment benefit plans under which an entity pays fixed contributions into a separate entity (a fund) and will have no legal or constructive obligation to pay further contributions if the fund does not hold sufficient assets to pay all employee benefits relating to employee service in the current and prior periods.

Defined benefit plans are postemployment benefit plans other than defined contribution plans.

Multiemployer plans are defined contribution plans (other than state plans) or defined benefit plans (other than state plans) that:

- (a) Pool the assets contributed by various entities that are not under common control
- (b) Use those assets to provide benefits to employees of more than one entity, on the basis that contribution and benefit levels are determined without regard to the identity of the entity that employs the employees concerned

Composite social security programs are established by legislation. They operate as multiemployer plans to provide postemployment benefits and provide benefits that are not consideration in exchange for service rendered by employees.

Plan assets comprise a) assets held by a long-term employee benefit fund and b) qualifying insurance policies.

Actuarial gains and losses comprise:

- (a) Experience adjustments (the effects of differences between the previous actuarial assumptions and what has actually occurred)
- (b) The effects of changes in actuarial assumptions

The **present value of a defined benefit obligation** is the present value, without deducting any plan assets, of expected future payments required to settle the obligation resulting from employee service in the current and prior periods.

Scope

IPSAS 25 must be applied by an employer in accounting for employee benefits. IPSAS 25 does not cover share-based transactions (cf. IPSAS 25.2). The relevant national or international accounting standards dealing with share-based transactions are applicable to such transactions. Equally, the standard does not deal with reporting by employee retirement benefit plans.

The standard deals (analogous to IAS 19) with four categories of employee benefits (cf. IPSAS 25.5):

1. **Short-term employee benefits:** such as wages, salaries and social security contributions, paid annual leave and paid sick leave, profit-sharing and bonuses (if payable within 12 months of the end of the period) and non-monetary benefits (such as medical care, housing, cars and free or subsidized goods or services) for current employees

2. **Postemployment benefits:** such as pensions, other retirement benefits, postemployment life insurance and postemployment medical care

3. **Other long-term employee benefits:** which may include long-service leave or sabbatical leave, jubilee or other long-service benefits, long-term disability benefits and, if they are not payable wholly within 12 months after the end of the period, profit-sharing, bonuses and deferred compensation

4. **Termination benefits**

Accounting for short-term employee benefits

Short-term employee benefits under IPSAS 25.11 include items such as:

(a) Wages, salaries and social security contributions

(b) Short-term compensated absences (such as paid annual leave and paid sick leave) where the absences are expected to occur within 12 months after the end of the period in which the employees render the related employee service

(c) Performance related bonuses and profit-sharing payable within 12 months after the end of the period in which the employees render the related service

(d) Non-monetary benefits (such as medical care, housing, cars and free or subsidized goods or services) for current employees

According to IPSAS 25.13, when an employee has rendered service to an entity during an accounting period, the entity must recognize the undiscounted amount of short-term employee benefits expected to be paid in exchange for that service:

    (a) As a liability (accrued expense), after deducting any amount already paid. If the amount already paid exceeds the undiscounted amount of the benefits, an entity must recognize that excess as an asset (prepaid expense) to the extent that the prepayment will lead to, for example, a reduction in future payments or a cash refund

    (b) As an expense, unless another standard requires or permits the inclusion of the benefits in the cost of an asset (cf., for example, IPSAS 12, "Inventories", and IPSAS 17, "Property, Plant and Equipment")

Pursuant to IPSAS 25.14, an entity must recognize the expected cost of short-term employee benefits in the form of **compensated absences** as follows:

    (a) In the case of accumulating compensated absences, when the employees render service that increases their entitlement to future compensated absences

    (b) In the case of non-accumulating compensated absences, when the absences occur

An entity must measure the expected cost of **accumulating compensated absences** as the additional amount that the entity expects to pay as a result of the unused entitlement that has accumulated at the reporting date (cf. IPSAS 25.17).

According to IPSAS 25.20, an entity must recognize the expected cost of **bonus payments** and **profit-sharing payments** (pursuant to IPSAS 25.13) when, and only when

    (a) The entity has a present legal or constructive obligation to make such payments as a result of past events

    (b) A reliable estimate of the obligation can be made

A present obligation exists when, and only when, the entity has no realistic alternative but to make the payments.

Accounting for postemployment benefits

a) Defined benefit versus defined contribution plans

According to IPSAS 25.27, **postemployment benefits** include, for example:

(a) Retirement benefits, such as pensions

(b) Other postemployment benefits, such as postemployment life insurance and postemployment medical care

Arrangements under which an entity provides postemployment benefits are **postemployment benefit plans**. An entity applies IPSAS 25 to all such arrangements whether or not they involve the establishment of a separate entity (a fund) to receive contributions and to pay benefits.

According to IPSAS 25, postemployment benefit plans are classified as either **defined contribution plans** or **defined benefit plans**, depending on the economic substance of the plan as derived from its principal terms and conditions (cf. IPSAS 25.28).

Defined contribution plans are postemployment benefit plans under which an entity pays fixed contributions into a separate entity (a fund) and will have no legal or constructive obligation to pay further contributions if the fund does not hold sufficient assets to pay all employee benefits relating to employee service in the current and prior periods (cf. IPSAS 25.28).

Thus, the amount of the postemployment benefits received by the employee is determined by the amount of contributions paid by an entity (and perhaps also the employee) to a postemployment benefit plan or to an insurance company, together with return on investment arising from the contributions. In consequence, actuarial risk (that benefits will be less than expected) and investment risk (that assets invested will be insufficient to meet expected benefits) are borne by the employee.

All other postemployment benefit plans are **defined benefit plans**. Under defined benefit plans (cf. IPSAS 25.30):

(a) The entity's obligation is to provide the agreed benefits to current and former employees.

(b) Actuarial risk (that benefits will cost more than expected) and investment risk are borne, in substance, by the entity. If actuarial or investment experience are worse than expected, the entity's obligation may be increased.

b) Treatment of multi-employer plans

An entity classifies a **multi-employer plan** as a defined contribution plan or a defined benefit plan under the terms of the plan (including any constructive obligation that goes beyond the formal terms) (cf. IPSAS 25.32). Where a multi-employer plan is a defined benefit plan, an entity must:

(a) Account for its proportionate share of the defined benefit obligation, plan assets and cost associated with the plan in the same way as for any other defined benefit plan

(b) Disclose the information required by IPSAS 25.141

When sufficient information is not available to use defined benefit accounting for a multi-employer plan that is a defined benefit plan, an entity must, pursuant to IPSAS 25.33:

(a) Account for the plan under IPSAS 25.55-57 (see below) as if it were a defined contribution plan

(b) Disclose:

(i) The fact that the plan is a defined benefit plan

(ii) The reason why sufficient information is not available to enable the entity to account for the plan as a defined benefit plan

(c) To the extent that a surplus or deficit in the plan may affect the amount of future contributions, the entity must disclose in addition:

(i) Any available information about that surplus or deficit

(ii) The basis used to determine that surplus or deficit

(iii) The implications, if any, for the entity

An entity must account for postemployment benefits under state plans or composite social security programs in the same way as for a multi-employer plan (cf. IPSAS 25.43 and 25.47).

c) Accounting for defined contribution plans

Accounting for defined contribution plans is straightforward because the reporting entity's obligation for each period is determined by the amounts to be contributed for that period (cf. IPSAS 25.54). Consequently, no actuarial assumptions are required to measure the obligation or the expense and there is no possibility of any actuarial gain or loss. Moreover, the obligations are measured on an undiscounted basis, except where they do not fall due wholly within 12 months of the end of the period in which the employees render the related service.

When an employee has rendered service to the entity during a period, the entity must recognize the contribution payable to defined contribution plan in exchange for that service (cf. IPSAS 25.56):

(a) As a liability (accrued expense), after deducting any contribution already paid. If the contribution already paid exceeds the contribution due for service before the reporting date, an entity must recognize that excess as an asset (prepaid expense) to the extent that prepayment will lead to, for example, a reduction in future payments or cash refund.

(b) As an expense, unless another IPSAS requires or permits the inclusion of the benefits in the cost of an asset (cf., for example, IPSAS 12 "Inventories" and IPSAS 17 "Property, Plant and Equipment").

Where contributions to a defined contribution plan do not fall due wholly within 12 months of the end of the period in which the employees render the related service, they should be discounted using the discount rate specified in IPSAS 25.91 (cf. IPSAS 25.55).

d) Accounting for defined benefit plans and determining the present value of defined benefit obligations

Accounting for defined benefit plans is complex because actuarial assumptions are required to measure the obligation and the expense and there is a possibility of actuarial gains and losses (cf. IPSAS 25.59). Moreover, the obligations are measured on a discounted basis because they may be settled many years after the employees render the related service.

An entity must account not only for its legal obligation under the formal terms of a defined benefit plan, but also for any constructive obligation that arises from the entity's informal practices (cf. IPSAS 25.63). Informal practices give rise to a constructive obligation where the entity has no realistic alternative but to pay employee benefits. An example of a constructive obligation is where a change in the entity's informal practices would cause unacceptable damage to its relationship with employees.

Pursuant to IPSAS 25.65, the amount recognized as a defined benefit liability is the net total of the following amounts:

(a) The present value of the defined benefit obligation at the reporting date (cf. IPSAS 25.77)

(b) Plus any actuarial gains (less any actuarial losses) not recognized because of the treatment set out in IPSAS 25.105-106

    (c) Minus any past service cost not yet recognized (cf. IPSAS 25.112)

    (d) Minus the fair value at the reporting date of plan assets (if any) out of which the obligations are to be settled directly (cf. IPSAS 25.118-120)

An entity must determine the **present value of defined benefit obligations** and the fair value of any plan assets with sufficient regularity that the amounts recognized in the financial statements do not differ materially from the amounts that would be determined at the reporting date.

Pursuant to IPSAS 25.74, for a defined benefit plan an entity must recognize the net total of the following amounts in surplus or deficit, unless another IPSAS requires or permits their inclusion in the cost of an asset:

    (a) Current service post (cf. IPSAS 25.76-104)

    (b) Interest cost (cf. IPSAS 25.95)

    (c) The expected return on any plan assets (cf. IPSAS 25.125-127) and on any reimbursement rights (cf. IPSAS 25.121)

    (d) Actuarial gains and losses, to the extent that they are recognized under IPSAS 25.105-109

    (e) Past service cost (cf. IPSAS 25.112)

    (f) The effect of the limit in IPSAS 25.65(b), unless it is recognized in the statement of changes in net assets/equity

Actuarial assumptions used in determining the present value of defined benefit obligations must be unbiased and mutually compatible (cf. IPSAS 25.85). Actuarial assumptions are an entity's best estimates of the variables that will determine the ultimate cost of providing postemployment benefits. Actuarial assumptions comprise demographic assumptions about the future characteristics of current and former employees (and their dependants) that are eligible for benefits. Factors used to determine these assumptions include, for example, the mortality of the recipients or rates of employee turnover. Financial assumptions, such as the discount rate or future salary and benefit levels, must also be made. Financial assumptions should be based on market expectations, at the reporting sheet date, for the period over which the obligations are to be settled.

The **rate** used to discount postemployment benefit obligations (both funded and unfunded) should reflect the time value of money (cf. IPSAS 25.91). The currency and term of the financial instrument selected to reflect the time value of money must be consistent with the currency and the estimated term of the postemployment benefit obligations.

The fair value of any **plan assets** is deducted in determining the amount recognized in the statement of financial position under IPSAS 25.65 (cf. IPSAS 25.118). When no market price is available, the fair value of plan assets is estimated, for example, by discounting expected future cash flows using a discount rate that reflects both the risk associated with the plan assets and the maturity or expected disposal date of those assets (or, if they have no maturity, the expected period until the settlement of the related obligation).

Other long-term employee benefits

According to IPSAS 25.147, **other long-term employee benefits** include, for example:

(a) Long-term compensated absences such as long-service or sabbatical leave

(b) Jubilee or other long-service benefits

(c) Long-term disability benefits

(d) Bonuses and profit-sharing payable 12 months or more after the end of the period in which the employees render the related service

(e) Deferred compensation paid 12 months or more after the end of the period in which it is earned

(f) Compensation payable by the entity until an individual enters new employment

Pursuant to IPSAS 25.150, the amount recognized as a liability for other long-term employee benefits should be the net total of the following amounts:

(a) The present value of the defined benefit obligation at the reporting date (cf. IPSAS 25.77)

(b) Minus the fair value at the reporting date of plan assets (if any) out of which the obligations are to be settled directly (cf. IPSAS 25.120-124)

In measuring the liability, an entity must apply IPSAS 25.55-104, excluding IPSAS 25.65 and IPSAS 25.74. An entity must apply IPSAS 25.121 in recognizing and measuring any reimbursement right.

For other long-term employee benefits, an entity must recognize the net total of the following amounts as expense or (subject to IPSAS 25.69) revenue, except to the extent that another standard requires or permits their inclusion in the cost of an asset:

(a) Current service cost (cf. IPSAS 25.76-104)

(b) Interest cost (cf. IPSAS 25.95)

(c) The expected return on any plan assets (cf. IPSAS 25.125-127) and on any reimbursement right recognized as an asset (cf. IPSAS 25.121)

(d) Actuarial gains and losses, which must all be recognized immediately

(e) Past service cost, which must all be recognized immediately

(f) The effect of any curtailments or settlements (cf. IPSAS 25.129-130)

Accounting for termination benefits

IPSAS 25 deals with **termination benefits** separately from other employee benefits because the event which gives rise to an obligation is the termination rather than employee service.

IPSAS 25.155 states that an entity must recognize termination benefits as a liability and an expense when, and only when, the entity is demonstrably committed to either:

(a) Terminate the employment of an employee or group of employees before the normal retirement date

(b) Provide termination benefits as a result of an offer made in order to encourage voluntary redundancy

Where termination benefits fall due more than 12 months after the reporting date, they must be discounted using the discount rate specified in IPSAS 25.91 (cf. IPSAS 25.161).

Effective date

Periods beginning on or after 1 January 2011.

IPSAS 26: Impairment of Cash-Generating Assets

Objective

The objective of IPSAS 26 is to prescribe the procedures that an entity applies to determine whether a cash-generating asset is impaired and to ensure that impairment losses are recognized. The standard also specifies when an entity should reverse an impairment loss and prescribes the necessary disclosures.

The IFRS on which the IPSAS is based

IAS 36 "Impairment of Assets" generally corresponds to IPSAS 26. However, because IPSAS 26 relates solely to cash-generating assets, IAS 36 and IPSAS 26 do not correspond in full.

Content

Principal definitions

Cash-generating assets are assets held with the primary objective of generating a commercial return.

A **cash-generating unit** is the smallest identifiable group of assets held with the primary objective of generating a commercial return that generates cash inflows from continuing use that are largely independent of the cash inflows from other assets or groups of assets.

An **impairment loss of a cash-generating asset** is the amount by which the carrying amount of an asset exceeds its recoverable amount.

The **recoverable amount** of an asset or a cash-generating unit is the higher of its fair value less costs to sell and its value in use.

Value in use of a cash-generating asset is the present value of the estimated future cash flows expected to be derived from the continuing use of an asset and from its disposal at the end of its useful life.

Scope

IPSAS 26 applies to all cash-generating assets with the exception of assets arising from construction contracts (cf. IPSAS 11), inventories (cf. IPSAS 12), financial assets that are within the scope of IPSAS 15, investment property that is measured at fair value (cf. IPSAS 16), cash-generating property, plant and equipment that is measured at revalued amounts (cf. IPSAS 17), deferred tax assets (in accordance with the national and international provisions), assets arising from employee benefits (cf. IPSAS

151

25), intangible assets that are regularly revalued to fair value and other assets listed in IPSAS 26.2.

Non-cash-generating assets, i.e., assets not held with the primary objective of generating a commercial return, are dealt with in IPSAS 21 "Impairment of Non-Cash-Generating Assets".

Carrying out an impairment test

IPSAS 26.22 states that an entity must assess at each reporting date whether there is any indication that an asset may be impaired. If any such indication exists, the entity must estimate the recoverable amount of the asset. The criteria used to assess whether there is any indication that an asset may be impaired are provided in IPSAS 26.25.

Irrespective of whether there is any indication of impairment, an entity must also test an **intangible asset** with an indefinite useful life or an intangible asset not yet available for use for impairment annually by comparing its carrying amount with its recoverable amount (cf. IPSAS 26.23). This impairment test may be performed at any time during the reporting period, provided it is performed at the same time every year. Different intangible assets may be tested for impairment at different times. However, if such an intangible asset was initially recognized during the current reporting period, that intangible asset must be tested for impairment before the end of that period.

In assessing whether there is any indication that an asset may be impaired, an entity must at least consider the **indications** listed in IPSAS 26.25. The standard distinguishes between external and internal sources of information (cf. IPSAS 26.25).

Measuring recoverable amount

The **recoverable amount of a cash-generating asset** is the higher of an asset's fair value less costs to sell and its value in use (cf. IPSAS 26.31). The **value in use** of a cash-generating asset is the present value of the estimated future cash flows expected to be derived from the continuing use of an asset and from its disposal at the end of its useful life. The elements listed in IPSAS 26.43, such as an estimate of the future cash flows the entity expects to derive from the asset or expectations about possible variations in the amount or timing of those future cash flows must be reflected in the calculation of an asset's value in use.

Recognizing and measuring an impairment loss

Pursuant to IPSAS 26.72, an **impairment loss** is recognized if, and only if, the recoverable amount of an asset is less than its carrying amount. In this case the carrying amount of the asset is reduced to its recoverable amount. The impairment loss is recognized immediately in surplus or deficit (cf. IPSAS 26.73).

After the recognition of an impairment loss, the depreciation (amortization) charge for the asset is adjusted in future periods to allocate the asset's revised carrying amount, less its residual value (if any), on a systematic basis over its remaining useful life (cf. IPSAS 26.75).

If there is any indication that an asset may be impaired, the recoverable amount is estimated for the individual asset. If it is not possible to estimate the recoverable amount of the individual asset, an entity must determine the recoverable amount of the cash-generating unit to which the asset belongs (the asset's cash-generating unit).

Cash-generating units

A **cash-generating unit** is the smallest identifiable group of assets a) held with the primary objective of generating a commercial return that b) generates cash inflows from continuing use that are c) largely independent of the cash inflows from other assets or groups of assets. The appendix to IPSAS 26 contains examples that explain how to determine a cash-generating unit.

If an active market exists for the output produced by an asset or group of assets, that asset or group of assets is identified as a cash-generating unit, even if some or all of the output is used internally (cf. IPSAS 26.81). If the cash inflows generated by any asset or cash-generating unit are affected by internal transfer pricing, an entity must use management's best estimate of future price(s) that could be achieved in arm's length transactions in estimating a) the future cash inflows used to determine the asset's or unit's value in use and b) the future cash outflows used to determine the value in use of any other assets or cash-generating units that are affected by the internal transfer pricing.

According to IPSAS 26.83, cash-generating units are identified consistently from period to period for the same asset or types of assets, unless a change is justified.

Recognizing an impairment loss for a cash-generating unit

An impairment loss is recognized for a cash-generating unit if, and only if, the recoverable amount of the unit is less than the carrying amount of the unit. The impairment loss is allocated to reduce the carrying amount of cash-generating assets of the unit on a pro rata basis, based on the carrying amount of each asset in the unit. These reductions in carrying amounts are treated as impairment losses on individual assets and recognized in accordance with IPSAS 26.73.

In allocating an impairment loss for a cash-generating unit, an entity cannot reduce the carrying amount of an asset below the highest of (cf. IPSAS 26.92):

(a) Its fair value less costs to sell (if determinable)

(b) Its value in use (if determinable)

(c) Zero

The amount of the impairment loss that would otherwise have been allocated to the asset is allocated pro rata to the other cash-generating assets of the unit.

After the requirements in IPSAS 26.91-93 have been applied, a liability is recognized for any remaining amount of an impairment loss for a cash-generating unit if, and only if, that is required by another IPSAS (cf. IPSAS 26.97).

Reversing an impairment loss

As far as reversing an impairment loss recorded on an asset or a cash-generating unit in earlier reporting periods is concerned, an entity must assess at each reporting date whether there is any indication that an impairment loss recognized in prior periods for an asset may no longer exist or may have decreased (cf. IPSAS 26.99). This means that there is a **duty to reverse impairment losses**.

If any such indication exists, the entity must estimate the recoverable amount of the asset. The comments in IPSAS 26.100 are applicable in assessing whether there is any such indication. An impairment loss recognized in prior periods for an asset is reversed if, and only if, there has been a change in the estimates used to determine the asset's recoverable amount since the last impairment loss was recognized (cf. IPSAS 26.103). If this is the case, the carrying amount of the asset is increased to its recoverable amount (reversal of impairment loss).

The increased carrying amount of an asset due to a reversal of an impairment loss cannot exceed the carrying amount that would have been determined (net of amortization or depreciation) had no impairment loss been recognized for the asset in prior years (cf. IPSAS 26.106). A reversal of an impairment loss for an asset is recognized immediately in surplus or deficit pursuant to IPSAS 26.106.

After a reversal of an impairment loss is recognized, the depreciation (amortization) charge for the asset is adjusted in future periods to allocate the asset's revised carrying amount, less its residual value (if any), on a systematic basis over its remaining useful life (cf. IPSAS 26.109).

A **reversal of an impairment loss for a cash-generating unit** is allocated to the cash-generating assets of the unit pro rata with the carrying amounts of those assets (cf. IPSAS 26.110). These increases in carrying amounts are treated as reversals of impairment losses for individual assets and recognized in accordance with IPSAS 26.109. No part of the amount of such a reversal is allocated to a non-cash-generating asset contributing service potential to a cash-generating unit.

In allocating a reversal of impairment loss for a cash-generating unit as described above, the carrying amount of an asset cannot be increased above the lower of (cf. IPSAS 26.111):

(a) Its recoverable amount (if determinable)

(b) The carrying amount that would have been determined (net of amortization or depreciation) had no impairment loss been recognized for the asset in prior periods

The amount of the reversal of the impairment loss that would otherwise have been allocated to the asset is allocated pro rata to the other assets of the unit.

Redesignation of cash-generating and non-cash-generating assets

The redesignation of an asset from a cash-generating asset to a non-cash-generating asset or from a non-cash-generating asset to a cash-generating asset can only occur when there is clear evidence that such a redesignation is appropriate. A redesignation, by itself, does not necessarily trigger an impairment test or a reversal of an impairment loss. At the subsequent reporting date after a redesignation, an entity must at least consider the listed indications in IPSAS 26.25.

Disclosure requirements

An entity must disclose the criteria developed by the entity to distinguish cash-generating assets from non-cash-generating assets.

Further disclosure requirements in relation to cash-generating assets and cash-generating units can be found in IPSAS 115 et seq.

Effective date

Periods beginning on or after 1 April 2009.

IV   Overview of current Exposure Drafts

Objective

ED 36 prescribes the accounting treatment and disclosures related to agricultural activity. Among other things, it deals with the accounting treatment for biological assets during the period of growth, degeneration, production, and procreation, and for the initial measurement of agricultural produce at the point of harvest.

The IFRS on which the IPSAS will be based

IAS 41 "Agriculture"

Content

Principal definitions

Agricultural activity is the management by an entity of the biological transformation and harvest of biological assets for sale, including exchange or non-exchange transactions, or for conversion into agricultural produce, or into additional biological assets. Agricultural activity covers such activities as raising livestock, forestry, annual or perennial cropping, cultivating orchards and plantations, floriculture, and aquaculture (including fish farming). ED 36.9 lists certain common features of agricultural activities.

Agricultural produce is the harvested product of the entity's biological assets, whereas a **biological asset** is a living animal or plant.

Biological transformation comprises the processes of growth, degeneration, production, and procreation that cause qualitative or quantitative changes in a biological asset. Biological transformation results in the following types of outcomes:

(a) Asset changes through

  (i) Growth (an increase in quantity or improvement in quality of an animal or plant),

  (ii) Degeneration (a decrease in the quantity or deterioration in quality of an animal or plant), or

  (iii) Procreation (creation of additional living animals or plants); or

157

(b) Production of agricultural produce such as latex, tea leaf, wool, and milk.

Costs to sell are the incremental costs directly attributable to the disposal of an asset, excluding finance costs and income taxes.

The following table shows examples of biological assets, agricultural produce, and products that are the result of processing after harvest:

Biological assets	Agricultural produce	Products that are the result of processing after harvest
Dairy cattle	Milk	Cheese
Fruit trees	Picked fruit	Processed fruit
Vines	Grapes	Wine

Table 16: Examples of biological assets, agricultural produce and products that are the result of processing after harvest

Scope

A public sector entity using the accrual basis of accounting is to apply the forthcoming standard for **biological assets** and **agricultural produce** at the point of harvest when they relate to **agricultural activity**. After the point of harvest, IPSAS 12 "Inventories" or another applicable standard is used. The proposed standard will <u>not</u> deal with the processing of agricultural produce after harvest; for example, the processing of picked tea leaves into tea by a farmer who has grown the tea bushes. Also, the forthcoming standard will not apply to:

(a) Land related to agricultural activity (cf. IPSAS 16 and IPSAS 17)

(b) Intangible assets related to agricultural activity

(c) Biological assets held for the supply of (public) services

Recognition of biological assets and agricultural produce

According to ED 36.13 an entity may recognize a biological asset or agricultural produce when and only when:

(a) The entity controls the asset as a result of past events;

(b) It is probable that future economic benefits or service potential associated with the asset will flow to the entity; and

(c) The fair value or cost of the asset can be measured reliably.

The recognition criteria refer to the definition of an asset as prescribed in IPSAS 1. In agricultural activity, control may be substantiated by legal ownership and the branding. The future benefits or service potential in agricultural activity are normally assessed by measuring the significant physical attributes.

Measurement of biological assets and agricultural produce

ED 36.15 prescribes that a **biological asset** be measured on initial recognition and at each reporting date at its fair value less costs to sell, except where the fair value cannot be measured reliably. For subsequent measurement, ED 36.34 states that an entity that has previously measured a biological asset at its fair value less costs to sell continues to measure the biological asset at its fair value less costs to sell until disposal.

According to ED 36.16 **agricultural produce** harvested from an entity's biological assets is measured at its fair value less costs to sell at the point of harvest. This measurement will be the cost at that date when applying IPSAS 12 "Inventories" or another applicable standard. In the determination of cost, accumulated depreciation and accumulated impairment losses, the entity is also required to consider IPSAS 12 "Inventories," IPSAS 17 "Property, Plant and Equipment", IPSAS 21 "Impairment of Non-Cash-Generating Assets" as well as IPSAS 26 "Impairment of Cash-Generating Assets (cf. ED 36.35).

Contrary to biological assets, agricultural produce harvested from an entity's biological assets will be measured at its fair value less costs to sell only **at the point of harvest**. ED 36.34 indicates that there are no exceptions to the rule of measuring agricultural produce at the point of harvest at its fair value less costs to sell. The proposed standard assumes that the fair value of agricultural produce at the point of harvest can always be measured reliably. To conclude, the primary measurement basis for biological assets and agricultural produce is fair value.

Determination of fair value for a biological asset or agricultural produce

ED 36.12 states that the fair value of an asset is based on its present location and condition. As a result, for example, the fair value of cattle at a farm is the price for the cattle in the relevant market less the transport and other costs of getting the cattle to that market.

If an active market exists for a biological asset or agricultural produce in its present location and condition, the quoted price in that market is the appropriate basis for determining the fair value of that asset (cf. ED 36.19). If an entity has access to different active markets, the entity uses the most relevant one. For example, if an entity has access to two active markets, it would use the price existing in the market expected to be used.

If there is no active market, ED 36.20 proposes that an entity use one or more of the following as reference for determining fair value:

(a) The most recent market transaction price, provided that there has not been a significant change in economic circumstances between the date of that transaction and the reporting date

(b) Market prices for similar assets with adjustment to reflect differences

(c) Sector benchmarks such as the value of an orchard expressed per export tray, bushel, or hectare, and the value of cattle expressed per kilogram of meat

The determination of fair value for a biological asset or agricultural produce may be facilitated by **grouping** biological assets or agricultural produce according to significant attributes, for example, by age or quality. The entity selects the attributes corresponding to the attributes used in the market as a basis for pricing (cf. ED 36.17).

Measurement of a biological asset

a) Determination of fair value if market prices are not available

In some circumstances, market-determined prices or values may not be available for a biological asset in its present condition. In determining fair value in these circumstances, an entity uses the **present value of expected net cash flows** from the asset discounted at a current market-determined rate. For the determination of the present value of expected net cash flows, ED 36.23 provides that entities should include the net cash flows that market participants would expect the asset to generate in its most relevant market. By contrast, cash flows for financing the assets, taxation, or re-establishing biological assets after harvest (for example, the cost of replanting trees in a plantation forest after harvest) are not included (cf. ED 36.24).

Furthermore, there are circumstances where **cost** may approximate fair value, particularly when:

(a) Little biological transformation has taken place since initial cost incurrence (for example, for vegetable seedlings planted immediately prior to reporting date); or

(b) The impact of the biological transformation on price is not expected to be material (for example, for the initial growth in a 30-year pine plantation production cycle).

b) Measurement when fair value cannot be measured reliable

If the fair value of a biological asset cannot be measured reliably on initial recognition, i.e., market-determined prices or values are not available and alternative estimates of fair value are determined to be clearly unreliable, then the biological asset is required to be measured at its cost less any accumulated depreciation and any accumulated impairment losses. Once the fair value of the respective biological asset becomes reliably measurable, the entity measures it at its fair value less costs to sell. Where a non-current biological asset (e.g., diary livestock) meets the criteria to be classified as held for sale in accordance with the relevant international or national accounting standard dealing with non-current assets held for sale and discontinued operations, it is presumed that fair value can be measured reliably.

Accounting treatment of gains or losses

a) Gains or losses arising on initial recognition

According to ED 36.28 and 36.30, a gain or loss arising on initial recognition of a biological asset or agricultural produce at fair value less costs to sell is included in surplus or deficit for the period in which it arises. A gain arising on initial recognition of a biological asset may arise, e.g., when a calf is born (cf. ED 36.29). A gain or loss may arise on initial recognition of agricultural produce as a result of harvesting (cf. ED 36.31).

b) Gains or losses from a change in fair value less costs to sell

By analogy to gains or losses arising on initial recognition, ED 36.28 states that gains or losses arising from a change in fair value less costs to sell of a biological asset should be included in surplus or deficit for the period in which it arises. Therefore, the change in fair value less costs to sell of a biological asset will have a direct impact on the statement of financial performance.

Government grants related to biological assets

IAS 41 contains requirements and guidance for accounting for government grants related to biological assets measured at fair value less costs to sell and agricultural activity. The IPSASB decided not to include requirements and guidance for government grants in ED 36 because IPSAS 23 "Revenue from Non-Exchange Transactions" sets forth requirements and guidance related to government grants provided in non-exchange transactions.

Effective date

To be determined.

IPSAS ED 37: Financial Instruments: Presentation

Preliminary note

It is proposed that ED 37 replace IPSAS 15 "Financial Instruments: Presentation and Disclosure" (issued December 2001), in accordance with the IPSASB's strategic aim of converging public sector accounting standards with IFRSs to the extent appropriate. ED 37 was published in April 2009 as an integrated package with IPSAS ED 38 "Financial Instruments: Recognition and Measurement", and IPSAS ED 39 "Financial Instruments: Disclosures".

Objective

The ED proposes principles for presenting financial instruments. Financial instruments are classified as financial assets, financial liabilities and equity instruments. In addition, it applies to the classification of related interest, dividends or similar distributions as well as losses and gains relating to a financial instrument. Furthermore the ED describes the circumstances in which financial assets and financial liabilities should be offset.

The IFRS on which the IPSAS will be based

IAS 32 "Financial Instruments: Presentation" (revised 2008)

Content

Principal definitions (cf. ED 37.9 for more details)

A **financial instrument** is any contract that gives rise to a financial asset of one entity and a financial liability or equity instrument of another entity.

A **financial asset** is any asset that is cash, an equity instrument of another entity or a contractual right to receive cash or another financial asset.

A **financial liability** is any liability that is a contractual obligation to deliver cash or another financial asset.

An **equity instrument** is any contract that evidences a residual interest in the assets of an entity after deducting all of its liabilities.

Scope

Excluded from the scope of ED 37 are interests in controlled entities (IPSAS 6), associates (IPSAS 7) or joint ventures (IPSAS 8) that are measured in an entity's financial statements using cost or the equity method, employers' rights and obligations under employee benefit plans (IPSAS 25), obligations

163

arising from insurance contracts (but note the exceptions) and share-based payment transactions.

Presentation of liabilities and equity

The issuer shall classify a financial instrument on initial recognition in accordance with the substance of the contractual arrangement as a financial liability, a financial asset or an equity instrument (**substance over form**). A critical feature in distinguishing a financial liability from an equity instrument is the existence of a contractual obligation to deliver either cash or another financial asset.

The scope of ED 37 excludes insurance contracts but deals with financial guarantee contracts and with insurance contracts that transfer financial risk. **Financial guarantee contracts** are contracts that require the issuer to make specified payments to reimburse the holder for a loss it incurs because a specified debtor fails to make payment when due in accordance with the original terms of a debt instrument. ED 37 distinguishes financial guarantee contracts arising from non-exchange transactions (i.e., at no consideration or nominal consideration) and financial guarantee contracts arising from exchange transactions. Financial guarantee contracts issued by way of non-exchange transactions are required to be treated as financial instruments in accordance with ED 37, whereas financial guarantee contracts issued by way of exchange transactions lead to an option. They should be treated as financial instruments unless an issuer elects to treat such contracts as insurance contracts (e.g., in accordance with IFRS 4). Contracts that are **insurance contracts but involve the transfer of financial risk** may be treated as financial instruments in accordance with ED 37.

Presentation of interest, dividends, losses and gains

Interest, dividends, losses and gains relating to a financial instrument that is a financial liability are recognized as revenue or expense in surplus or deficit. Distributions to holders of an equity instrument are debited directly to net assets/equity.

Offsetting a financial asset and a financial liability

Financial assets and financial liabilities shall be offset when an entity has a legally enforceable right to set off and intends either to settle on a net basis, or to realize the asset and settle the liability simultaneously.

Effective date

To be determined.

IPSAS ED 38: Financial Instruments: Recognition and Measurement

Objective

The objective of ED 38 is to propose requirements for the recognition and measurement of financial assets, financial liabilities and some contracts to buy or sell non-financial items.

The IFRS on which the IPSAS will be based

IAS 39 "Financial Instruments: Recognition and Measurement" (revised 2008)

Content

Principal definitions (cf. ED 38.10 for more details)

The terms **financial instrument**, financial asset, financial liability and equity instrument are defined in IPSAS ED 37. These terms are used in ED 38 with the same meaning.

ED 38 specifies **categories of financial instruments**. This classification is of importance because the accounting treatment for a particular financial instrument depends on its classification. ED 38 distinguishes between the following categories of financial assets and financial liabilities:

Financial assets	Financial liabilities
- Financial assets at fair value through surplus or deficit	- Financial liabilities at fair value through surplus or deficit
- Held-to-maturity investments	- Other financial liabilities
- Loans and receivables	
- Available-for-sale financial assets	

Table 17: Categories of financial assets and financial liabilities

Financial assets or **financial liabilities at fair value through surplus or deficit** are financial instruments that are either classified as held for trading, or are designated as such on initial recognition. A financial asset or a financial liability is classified as 'held for trading' if:

166

- It is acquired or incurred principally for the purpose of selling or repurchasing it in the near term;
- On initial recognition it is part of a portfolio of identified financial instruments that are managed together and for which there is evidence of a recent actual pattern of short-term profit-taking; or
- It is a derivative.

Held-to-maturity investments are non-derivative financial assets with fixed or determinable payments and fixed maturity, other than 'loans and receivables', for which there is a positive intention and ability to hold to maturity and which have not been designated as 'at fair value through surplus or deficit' or as 'available-for-sale'.

Loans and receivables are non-derivative financial assets with fixed or determinable payments that are not quoted in an active market, do not qualify as 'financial assets held for trading' and have not been designated as 'at fair value through surplus or deficit' or as 'available-for-sale'.

Available-for-sale financial assets are non-derivative financial assets that are not classified as 'financial assets at fair value through surplus or deficit', 'held-to-maturity investments' or 'loans and receivables' ('default' classification), or are designated as such.

Other financial liabilities are those liabilities that are not 'held for trading' or that have not been designated as 'at fair value through surplus or deficit'.

Designation

The decision to designate a financial asset or to designate a financial liability to a certain category ('at fair value through surplus or deficit' or 'available-for-sale') is similar to a choice of accounting policy because the accounting treatment for a particular financial instrument depends on its classification. However, designation as 'at fair value through surplus or deficit' or 'available-for-sale' is only permitted upon initial recognition. Furthermore in designating an instrument as at fair value through surplus or deficit, an entity needs to demonstrate that doing so results in more relevant information because either:

- It eliminates or significantly reduces a measurement or recognition inconsistency (accounting mismatch) that would otherwise arise, or
- A group of financial assets, financial liabilities or both is managed and its performance is evaluated on a fair value basis, or
- The instruments contain embedded derivates.

Recognition and derecognition

ED 38.16 provides for an entity to **recognize a financial asset or a financial liability** in its statement of financial position when, and only when, the entity becomes a party to the contractual provisions of the instrument.

Derecognition is the removal of a previously recognized financial asset or financial liability from an entity's statement of financial position. An entity derecognizes a financial asset when the contractual rights to the cash flows from the financial asset expire or are waived or an **entity transfers the financial asset** and the **transfer qualifies for derecognition** (cf. ED 38.19).

An **entity transfers a financial asset** if it either transfers the contractual right to receive the cash flows of the financial asset, or retains the contractual rights to receive the cash flows of the financial asset, but assumes a contractual obligation to pay the cash flows in an arrangement that meets the conditions in ED 38.21.

The **transfer qualifies for derecognition** if the entity transfers substantially all the risks and rewards of ownership of the financial asset. If the entity retains substantially all the risks and rewards of ownership, the entity continues to recognize the financial asset.

If the entity neither transfers nor retains substantially all the risks and rewards, the entity must determine whether it has retained control of the financial asset. If the entity has retained control, it continues to recognize the financial asset to the extent of its continuing involvement. If the entity has not retained control, it derecognizes the financial asset and recognizes separately as assets or liabilities any rights and obligations created or retained in the transfer.

Initial measurement

When a financial asset or financial liability is **recognized initially**, an entity is required to measure it at its fair value. In the case of a financial asset or financial liability not at fair value through surplus or deficit, an entity shall measure it at its fair value plus transaction costs that are directly attributable to the acquisition or issue of the financial asset or financial liability (cf. ED 38.45).

Concessionary loans pose particular accounting issues to the public sector (cf. ED 38.AG83 to AG89). They are granted to or received by an entity at below market terms. Examples of concessionary loans granted by public sector entities include loans to developing countries and farms as well as student loans. Entities may receive concessionary loans, for example, from development agencies and other government entities. Concessionary loans are

168

distinguished from the **waiver of debt**. This distinction is important because it affects whether the below market conditions are considered in the initial recognition or measurement of the loan rather than as part of the subsequent measurement or derecognition. Any differences between the transaction price of the concessionary loan and fair value of the loan at initial recognition are treated as follows:

- Where the concessionary loan is received by a public sector entity, the difference is accounted for in accordance with IPSAS 23.
- Where the concessionary loan is granted by a public sector entity, the difference is treated as an expense in surplus or deficit at initial recognition.

In the public sector, **contractual financial guarantees** are frequently provided for no consideration or for nominal consideration to further the entity's economic and social objectives (e.g., supporting infrastructure projects or corporate entities in times of economic distress). In many cases the transaction price related to a financial guarantee contract will not reflect fair value and recognition at such an amount would be an inaccurate reflection of the issuer's exposure to financial risk. At initial recognition, where no fee is charged or where the consideration is not fair value, an entity firstly considers whether the fair value can be obtained through observation of an active market (level one). Where there is no active market for a directly equivalent guarantee contract, entities should apply a mathematical valuation technique to obtain a fair value where this produces a reliable measure of fair value (level two). Alternatively (level three), initial recognition should be in accordance with IPSAS 19.

Subsequent measurement

For the purpose of **measuring a financial asset after initial recognition** the accounting treatment of a particular financial instrument depends on its classification:

- 'Financial assets at fair value through surplus or deficit' are measured at their fair values without any deduction for transaction costs they may incur on sale. Gains and losses are recognized in surplus or deficit.
- 'Loans and receivables' and 'held-to-maturity investments' are measured at amortized cost using the effective interest method. Gains or losses are recognized in surplus or deficit when the financial asset is derecognized or impaired.
- Available-for-sale financial assets whose fair value can be reliably measured are measured at their fair values without any deduction for

transaction costs that may be incurred on sale. Gains and losses regarding the fair value measurement are recognized directly in net assets/equity. Investments that do not have a quoted market price in an active market and whose fair value cannot be reliably measured are measured at cost. In both cases, impairment losses are recognized in surplus or deficit.

Also, the **subsequent measurement of financial liabilities** depends on its classification:

- Financial liabilities at fair value through surplus or deficit are measured at their fair value. Gains and losses are recognized in surplus or deficit.
- Other financial liabilities are measured at cost. Gains or losses are recognized in surplus or deficit when the financial liability is derecognized or impaired.

Accounting for hedging instruments

The ED contains guidelines on hedge accounting in ED 38.81-113.

Effective date

To be determined.

IPSAS ED 39: Financial Instruments: Disclosures

Objective

The objective of ED 39 is to require entities to provide disclosure requirements for financial assets, financial liabilities and net assets/equity, the risks associated with holding financial instruments, and the entity's strategy for mitigating those risks.

The IFRS on which the IPSAS will be based

IFRS 7 "Financial Instruments: Disclosures" (revised 2008)

Content

Principal definitions

The terms financial instrument, financial asset and financial liability are defined in IPSAS ED 37. Categories of financial instruments are specified in IPSAS ED 38. These terms and classifications are used in ED 39 with the same meaning.

Credit risk is the risk that one party to a financial instrument will cause a financial loss for the other party by failing to discharge an obligation.

Liquidity risk is the risk that an entity will encounter difficulty in meeting obligations associated with financial liabilities that are settled by delivering cash or another financial asset.

Loans payable are financial liabilities, other than short-term trade payables on normal credit terms.

Market risk is the risk that the fair value or future cash flows of a financial instrument will fluctuate because of changes in market prices.

Scope

ED 39 applies to recognized and unrecognized financial instruments. Recognized financial instruments include financial assets and financial liabilities that are within the scope of ED 38. Unrecognized financial instruments include some financial instruments that, although outside the scope of ED 38, are within the scope of this ED.

Overview

The disclosure requirements of the proposed IPSAS could be divided into financial statement disclosures resulting from financial instruments and risk disclosures resulting from financial instruments. The following table illustrates the different kinds of disclosure requirements in ED 39.

Financial statement disclosures resulting from financial instruments	**Risk disclosures resulting from financial instruments**
General disclosures for all entities	Disclosures on credit risks
Specific disclosures for all entities	Disclosures on liquidity risks
Specific disclosures for public sector entities	Disclosures on market risks

Table 18: Overview on the disclosure requirements of ED 39

Except for the specific disclosures for public sector entities, ED 39 does not contain any material differences to IFRS 7.

General disclosures for all entities

General disclosures, such as the carrying amounts of financial instruments by category, have to be provided in the statement of financial position or in the notes (cf. ED 39.10).

Again in the statement of financial performance or in the notes, all entities have to disclose items of revenue, expense and gains or losses resulting from financial instruments (cf. ED 39.23).

In addition, entities are required to disclose the significant accounting policies relevant to an understanding of their financial instruments (cf. ED 39.24).

Specific disclosures for all entities

An entity must provide additional specific disclosures if:

- Financial assets or financial liabilities have been designated as 'at fair value through surplus or deficit' (cf. ED 38);
- Financial assets have been reclassified;
- Financial assets have been transferred and do not qualify for derecognition;

- Financial assets have been pledged as collateral or are held as collateral;

- The impairment of financial assets has been recorded in a separate account;

- A compound financial instrument with multiple embedded derivatives has been issued;

- Defaults of loans payable or breaches of loan agreement terms have been occurred;

- Hedge accounting is applied; or

- Financial assets or financial liabilities have been recorded at fair values.

Specific disclosures for public sector entities

Concessionary loans are granted to or received by an entity on below market terms. Examples of concessionary loans granted by entities include loans to developing countries, small farms, student loans granted to qualifying students for tertiary education and housing loans granted to low income families.

Such loans are characteristic for the public sector and are often made to implement a government's or other public sector entity's social policies. The intention of a concessionary loan at the outset is to provide or receive resources on below market terms. For this reason the IPSASB concluded that more comprehensive disclosures are required by public sector entities in respect of concessionary loans and it has included additional disclosure requirements with respect to concessionary loans (cf. ED 39.36):

- A reconciliation between the opening and closing balance of the loans

- The nominal value of the loans at the end of the period

- The purpose and terms of the various types of loans

- The valuation assumptions

Disclosures on credit risks

Besides qualitative disclosures on the credit risks arising from financial assets, an entity has to quantify its credit risks. Specific disclosures by category of financial instrument are required in particular for financial assets that are either past due or impaired. Collateral and other credit enhancements obtained have to be named, quantified and explained.

Disclosures on liquidity risks

Besides qualitative disclosures on the liquidity risks arising from financial liabilities, an entity has to quantify its liquidity risks. A maturity analysis must be disclosed for derivative and non-derivative financial liabilities.

Disclosures on market risks

Besides qualitative disclosures on the market risks arising from financial instruments, an entity has to quantify its market risks. A sensitivity analysis is required to be disclosed for each type of market risk.

Effective date

To be determined.

IPSAS ED 40: Intangible Assets

Objective

The objective of ED 40 is to prescribe the accounting treatment for intangible assets that are not dealt with specifically in any other IPSAS. It requires an entity to recognize an intangible asset if, and only if, specified criteria are met, including the definition of an asset. ED 40 also specifies how to measure the carrying amount of intangible assets and requires specified disclosures about intangible assets.

The IFRS on which the IPSAS will be based

IAS 38 "Intangible Assets" (revised 2008)

Content

Principal definitions

Amortization is the systematic allocation of the depreciable amount of an intangible asset over its useful life.

Development is the application of research findings or other knowledge to a plan or design for the production of new or substantially improved materials, devices, products, processes, systems or services before the start of commercial production or use.

Depreciable amount is the cost of an asset, or other amount substituted for cost, less its residual value.

Development is the application of research findings or other knowledge to a plan or design for the production of new or substantially improved materials, devices, products, processes, systems or services before the start of commercial production or use.

Goodwill is an asset representing the future economic benefits or service potential arising from other assets acquired in an entity combination that are not individually identified and separately recognized (cf. ED 41 Appendix A).

An **impairment loss** is the amount by which the carrying amount of an asset exceeds its recoverable amount.

An **intangible asset** is an identifiable non-monetary asset without physical substance. Typical examples of intangible assets in the public sector are computer software, patents, copyrights and acquired import quotas.

175

Research is original and planned investigation undertaken with the prospect of gaining new scientific or technical knowledge and understanding.

Scope

The proposed IPSAS applies to, among other things, expenditure on advertising, training, start-up, research and development activities. Therefore, although these activities may result in an asset with physical substance (e.g., a prototype), the physical element of the asset is secondary to its intangible component, i.e., the knowledge embodied in it. Because of its focus on research and development, the proposed IPSAS on intangible assets will be of great relevance to public research institutions as well as to public universities and colleges.

ED 40 shall be applied in accounting for intangible assets, except:

- (a) Intangible assets that are within the scope of another standard
- (b) Financial assets, as defined in ED 37 "Financial Instruments: Presentation"
- (c) The recognition and measurement of exploration and evaluation assets
- (d) Expenditure on the development and extraction of minerals, oil, natural gas and similar non-regenerative resources
- (e) Intangible assets acquired in an entity combination from a non-exchange transaction,
- (f) The power to grant rights and the power to tax

The IPSASB concluded that the power to grant rights and the power to tax do not meet the existing definition of an asset as set out in IPSAS 1. It is proposed that ED 40 should not apply to such powers.

Recognition

An intangible asset is an identifiable non-monetary asset without physical substance. ED 40.21 states that an asset meets the **"identifiable" criterion** in the definition of an intangible asset when it:

- Is separable, i.e., capable of being separated or divided from the entity and sold, licensed, rented or exchanged, either individually or together with a related contract, asset or liability; or
- Arises from rights from binding arrangements (including rights from contracts or other legal rights), regardless of whether those rights are transferable or separable from the entity or from other rights and obligations.

The "identifiable" criterion is necessary because the intangible asset needs to be distinguished from goodwill. In addition, the "identifiable" criterion in ED 40.21 has been expanded (contrary to IAS 38) to include rights arising from binding arrangements (including rights from contracts or other legal rights).

Derived from the definition of (intangible) assets, **control** is a further condition for recognition of an (intangible) asset. According to ED 40.22 a public sector entity controls an asset if the entity has the power to obtain the future economic benefits or service potential flowing from the underlying resource and to restrict the access of others to those benefits or that service potential. Revenue from the sale of products or services, cost savings, or other benefits resulting from the use of the asset by the entity are examples for the future economic benefits or service potential flowing from an intangible asset.

Further **recognition criteria** for an intangible asset are described in ED 40.30-32. Accordingly, an intangible asset shall be recognized if, and only if:

- It is probable that the expected future economic benefits or service potential that are attributable to the asset will flow to the entity; and
- The cost or fair value of the asset, as appropriate, can be measured reliably.

An entity shall assess the probability of expected future economic benefits or service potential using reasonable and supportable assumptions that represent management's best estimate of the set of economic conditions that will exist over the useful life of the asset (cf. ED 40.32).

Internally generated goodwill is not recognized as an asset because it is not an identifiable resource (i.e., it is not separable nor does it arise from binding arrangements – including rights from contracts or other legal rights – controlled by the entity that can be measured reliably at cost (cf. IPSAS 40.57).

For the assessment whether an **internally generated intangible asset** meets the criteria for recognition, a public sector entity classifies the generation of the asset into a **research phase** and a **development phase** (cf. ED 40.61). If the research phase cannot be distinguished from the development phase, then the entity should treat the expenditure on that project as if it were incurred in the research phase only, i.e., the expenditure is expensed. Expenditures on an intangible asset arising from **research** (or from the **research phase** of an internal project) may not be recognized as an asset (cf. ED 40.63). ED 40.64 explains that in the research phase of an internal project, an entity cannot demonstrate that an intangible asset exists that will generate probable future economic benefits or service potential. Therefore, this expenditure is recognized as an expense when it is incurred.

In contrast to the research phase, the proposed standard requires recognition of an intangible asset in the **development phase** because the development phase of a project is further advanced than the research phase and the entity may be able to demonstrate that the asset will generate probable future economic benefits or service potential.

According to ED 40.66 an intangible asset arising from development (or from the development phase of an internal project) shall be recognized if, and only if, an entity can demonstrate all of the following:

(a) The technical feasibility of completing the intangible asset so that it will be available for use or sale

(b) Its intention to complete the intangible asset and use or sell it

(c) Its ability to use or sell the intangible asset

(d) How the intangible asset will generate probable future economic benefits or service potential

(e) The availability of adequate technical, financial and other resources to complete the development and to use or sell the intangible asset

(f) Its ability to measure reliably the expenditure attributable to the intangible asset during its development

To demonstrate how an intangible asset will generate probable future economic benefits or service potential, an entity assesses the future economic benefits or service potential to be received from the asset using the principles in either IPSAS 21 "Impairment of Non-Cash-Generating Assets" or IPSAS 26 "Impairment of Cash-Generating Assets" as appropriate (cf. ED 40.69).

According to ED 40.72, internally generated brands, mastheads, publishing titles, lists of customers or users of an entity's services and items similar in substance may not be recognized as intangible assets.

The regulations on **intangible heritage assets** (e.g., recordings of significant historical events or rights to use the likeness of a significant public person in postage stamps or collectible coins) are comparable to those in IPSAS 17 "Property, Plant and Equipment". Therefore, the proposed standard does not require an entity to recognize intangible heritage assets. If an entity does recognize intangible heritage assets, it must apply disclosure requirements and may, but is not required to, apply the measurement requirements of the proposed standard.

Initial measurement

In general, an intangible asset that is separately acquired through an exchange transaction is measured initially **at cost** (cf. ED 40.33). The cost of a separately acquired intangible asset comprises:

- Its purchase price, including import duties and non-refundable purchase taxes, after deducting trade discounts and rebates; and
- Any directly attributable cost of preparing the asset for its intended use.

If an intangible asset is acquired in an entity combination from an exchange transaction, the cost of that intangible asset is its **fair value** at the acquisition date (cf. ED 41.42). ED 41.43 adds that an acquirer recognizes at the acquisition date, separately from goodwill, an intangible asset of the acquiree, irrespective of whether the asset had been recognized by the acquiree before the entity combination from an exchange transaction. Therefore, the acquirer recognizes as an asset separately from goodwill an in-process research and development project of the acquiree if the project meets the definition of an intangible asset.

An intangible asset that is acquired free of charge, or for nominal consideration, through a non-exchange transaction is measured at its **fair value** at the date it is acquired (cf. ED 40.53). Examples of such intangible assets are airport landing rights, licenses to operate radio or television stations or import licenses. If for example a Nobel Prize winner bequeaths free of charge his or her personal papers, including the copyright to his or her publications to the national archives (which are a public sector entity), then these intangible assets should be measured at their fair value at the acquisition date.

Subsequent measurement

For subsequent measurement of an intangible asset, an entity has the choice to use the **cost model** or the **revaluation model** as its accounting policy (cf. ED 40.82). If an intangible asset is accounted for using the revaluation model, all the other assets in its class shall also be accounted for using the same model, unless there is no active market for those assets. The cost model and the revaluation model applied to intangible assets are similar to IPSAS 17.43 et seq.

An **intangible asset with a finite useful life is amortized**, while an intangible asset with an indefinite useful life is not. Therefore, an entity must assess whether the useful life of an intangible asset is finite or indefinite.

According to ED 40.107, the depreciable amount of an intangible asset with a finite useful life is allocated on a systematic basis over its useful life. Amortization begins when the asset is available for use. Amortization ceases at the earlier of the date that the asset is classified as held for sale and the date that the asset is derecognized. The amortization method used should reflect the pattern in which the asset's future economic benefits or service potential are expected to be consumed by the entity. If that pattern cannot be determined reliably, the straight-line method should be used.

An intangible asset should be regarded by the entity as having an indefinite useful life when, based on an analysis of all of the relevant factors, there is no foreseeable limit to the period over which the asset is expected to generate net cash inflows for, or provide service potential to, the entity (cf. ED 40.98). An **intangible asset with an indefinite useful life may not be amortized**. The useful life of an intangible asset that is not being amortized is reviewed each reporting period to determine whether events and circumstances continue to support an indefinite useful life assessment for that asset (impairment test). If they do not, the change in the useful life assessment from indefinite to finite is accounted for as a change in an accounting estimate in accordance with IPSAS 3.

Web site costs

Contrary to IAS 38, the proposed IPSAS on intangible assets contains application guidance on web site costs based on the Standing Interpretations Committee's Interpretation (SIC) 32 "Intangible Assets − Web Site Costs".

Effective date

To be determined.

IPSAS ED 41: Entity Combinations from Exchange Transactions

Objective

The objective of ED 41 is to propose the accounting treatment for entity combinations from exchange transactions. Principles and requirements are established for how an acquirer:

- Recognizes and measures the identifiable assets acquired, the liabilities assumed, non-controlling interest in the acquiree and the goodwill acquired or a gain from a bargain purchased; and
- Determines what information to disclose.

The IFRS on which the IPSAS will be based

IFRS 3 "Business Combinations" (revised 2008)

Content

Principal definitions

An **entity combination** is a transaction or other event in which an acquirer obtains control of one or more operations.

An **operation** is an integrated set of activities and assets that is conducted and managed for the purpose of achieving an entity's objectives, either by providing economic benefits or service potential.

The **acquirer** is the entity that obtains control of the acquiree.

Goodwill is an asset representing the future economic benefits or service potential arising from other assets acquired in an entity combination that are not individually identified and separately recognized.

Scope exclusion

The scope is limited to entity combinations arising from exchange transactions and where the entities are not under common control. ED 41 does not apply to:

- Entity combinations arising from a non-exchange transaction
- The formation of a joint venture
- The acquisition of an asset or a group of assets that does not constitute an operation
- A combination of entities or operations under common control

Core principle

An entity combination from an exchange transaction must be accounted for by applying the acquisition method. This method assumes an acquisition, which is why the underlying assets and liabilities are recognized instead of the acquired interests. Under ED 41 an acquirer of an operation recognizes the assets acquired and liabilities assumed at their acquisition-date fair values.

Identifying the acquirer

For each entity combination, one of the combining entities is identified as the acquirer (cf. ED 41.11). The guidance in IPSAS 6 shall be used to identify the acquirer.

Determining the acquisition date

The acquisition date is the date on which the acquirer obtains control of the acquiree (cf. ED 41.13). This is generally the date on which the acquirer legally transfers the consideration, acquires the assets and assumes the liabilities of the acquiree (closing date).

Recognition and initial measurement of assets and liabilities

The acquirer **recognizes**, separately from goodwill, the identifiable assets acquired, the liabilities assumed and any non-controlling interest in the acquiree (cf. ED 41.15). The identifiable assets and liabilities must meet the definitions of assets and liabilities in IPSAS 1 at the acquisition date. In addition the identifiable assets and liabilities must be part of what the acquirer and the acquiree exchanged in the entity combination transaction rather than the result of separate transactions.

Assets acquired and liabilities assumed are **measured** at their acquisition-date fair values (cf. ED 41.24). Non-controlling interests in the acquiree are measured either at fair value or at the non-controlling interest's proportionate share of the acquiree's identifiable net assets.

Exceptions to the recognition or measurement principles:

Exception to the recognition principle	Exception to the measurement principle
- **Contingent liabilities** are recognized if they are present obligations that arise from past events and their fair value can be measured reliably.	- **Reacquired rights** are measured on the basis of the remaining term. - **Assets held for sale** are measured in accordance with international or national accounting standards.

- Where the acquiree is liable for **income taxes**, the acquirer shall refer to international or national accounting standards dealing with income taxes.

- Liabilities relating to the acquiree's **employee benefit arrangements** are accounted in accordance with IPSAS 25.

- The acquirer recognizes an **indemnification asset** at the same time that it recognizes the indemnified item measured on the same basis as the indemnified item.

Table 19: Exceptions to the recognition or measurement principle in ED 41

Recognizing and measuring goodwill or a gain from a bargain purchase

The acquirer recognizes **goodwill** as of the acquisition date measured as the excess of (a) over (b) below:

a) The aggregate of the consideration transferred, the amount of any non-controlling interest in the acquiree and the acquirer's previously held equity interest in the acquiree

b) The net of the acquisition-date amounts of the identifiable assets acquired and the liabilities assumed

Occasionally, an acquirer will make a **bargain purchase**, which is an entity combination in which the amount in (b) exceeds the aggregate of the amounts in (a). Before recognizing a gain on a bargain purchase, the acquirer must reassess whether it has correctly identified all of the assets acquired and all of the liabilities assumed, and recognize any additional assets or liabilities that are identified in that review. If the excess remains, the acquirer recognizes the resulting gain in surplus or deficit on the acquisition date. In this case, the public sector entity discloses the amount of any gain recognized, the line item in the statement of financial performance in which the gain is recognized and a description of the reasons why the transaction resulted in a gain.

For **subsequent measurement** the acquirer measures goodwill at the amount recognized at the acquisition date less any accumulated impairment losses. Irrespective of whether there is any indication of impairment, a public sector entity shall test goodwill for impairment annually. For the purpose of impairment testing, goodwill acquired is allocated to cash-generating units. Each unit or group of units to which the goodwill is allocated must represent the lowest level within the public sector entity at which the goodwill is monitored for internal management purposes and may not be larger than an operating segment determined in accordance with IPSAS 18.

Subsequent measurement of assets and liabilities

A public sector entity shall subsequently measure and account for assets acquired, liabilities assumed or incurred and equity instruments issued in accordance with any other IPSAS that is applicable for those items. However, ED 41 provides guidance on subsequently measuring reacquired rights, contingent liabilities recognized as of the acquisition date, indemnification assets and contingent consideration (cf. ED 41.59 et seq.).

Effective date

To be determined.

V   Cash Basis IPSAS

Objective

The Cash Basis IPSAS prescribes the manner in which general purpose financial statements should be presented using the cash basis of accounting.

Information about the cash receipts, cash payments and cash balances of an entity is necessary for accountability purposes. It also provides input useful for assessments of the ability of the entity to generate adequate cash in the future and the likely sources and uses of cash. In making and evaluating decisions about the allocation of cash resources and the sustainability of the entity's activities, users require an understanding of the timing and certainty of cash receipts and cash payments.

Compliance with the requirements and recommendations of this standard ensures comprehensive and transparent financial reporting of the cash receipts, cash payments and cash balances of the entity. It also enhances comparability with the entity's own financial statements of previous periods and with the financial statements of other entities which adopt the cash basis of accounting.

The IFRS on which the IPSAS is based

The Cash Basis IPSAS is an IPSAS specifically for the public sector. As a result there is no IFRS equivalent.

Content

Principal definitions

Unlike IPSAS 2, the Cash Basis IPSAS defines **cash** as cash on hand, demand deposits and cash equivalents.

Similarly to IPSAS 2, **cash equivalents** are defined as short-term, highly liquid investments (with maturities of less than three months from the date of purchase) that are readily convertible to known amounts of cash and which are subject to an insignificant risk of changes in value.

Contrary to IPSAS 2, the Cash Basis IPSAS defines **cash flows** as inflows and outflows of cash.

185

Cash payments are defined as cash outflows and **cash receipts** are defined as cash inflows.

Structure of the Cash Basis IPSAS

The standard has two parts:

Part 1 is mandatory. It sets out the requirements which are applicable to all entities preparing general purpose financial statements under the cash basis of accounting. The requirements in this first part of the standard must be complied with by entities which claim to be reporting in accordance with the Cash Basis IPSAS: Financial Reporting Under the Cash Basis of Accounting.

Part 2 is not mandatory. It identifies additional accounting policies and disclosures that an entity is encouraged to adopt to enhance its financial accountability and the transparency of its financial statements. It includes explanations of alternative methods of presenting certain information.

Comments on 'external assistance' were added to both the mandatory and voluntary parts at the end of 2007.

Overview – part 1:

Scope

With the exception of Government Business Enterprises, all public sector entities which prepare and present financial statements under the cash basis of accounting should apply the standard.

An entity whose financial statements comply with the requirements of Part 1 should disclose that fact.

Financial reporting under the cash basis of accounting

The cash basis of accounting recognizes transactions and events only when cash (including cash equivalents) is received or paid by the entity. Financial statements prepared under the cash basis provide readers with information about the sources of cash raised during the period. They also provide information on the purposes for which cash was used and the cash balances at the reporting date. The measurement focus in the financial statements is balances of cash (including cash equivalents) and any changes.

Cash is **controlled** by an entity when the entity can use the cash for the achievement of its own objectives or otherwise benefit from the cash and exclude or regulate the access of others to that benefit. The IPSASB established this principle in paragraph 1.2.6 of the Cash Basis IPSAS, "Financial Reporting Under the Cash Basis of Accounting".

186

Presentation of the financial statements

Paragraph 1.3.4 of the Cash Basis IPSAS sets out a complete set of financial statements as:

(a) A statement of cash receipts and payments which recognizes all cash receipts, cash payments and cash balances controlled by the entity and separately identifies payments made by third parties on behalf of the entity

(b) Accounting policies and explanatory notes

(c) When the entity makes publicly available its approved budget, a comparison of budget and actual amounts either as a separate additional financial statement or as a budget column in the statement of cash receipts and payments

Structure of the statement of cash receipts and payments

According to Cash Basis IPSAS 1.3.12, the statement of cash receipts and payments should present the following amounts for the reporting period:

(a) Total cash receipts of the entity showing separately a sub-classification of total cash receipts using a classification basis appropriate to the entity's operations

(b) Total cash payments of the entity showing separately a sub-classification of total cash payments using a classification basis appropriate to the entity's operations

(c) Opening and closing cash balances of the entity

Total cash receipts and total cash payments, and cash receipts and cash payments for each sub-classification of cash receipt and payment should be reported on a gross basis (cf. Cash Basis IPSAS 1.3.13). Cash receipts and payments may be reported on a net basis when:

(a) They arise from transactions which the entity administers on behalf of other parties and which are recognized in the statement of cash receipts and payments

(b) They are for items in which the turnover is quick, the amounts are large and the maturities are short

Cash Basis IPSAS 1.3.19 and 1.3.20 contain further examples of transactions where cash receipts and payments can be reported on a net basis. Pursuant to Cash Basis IPSAS 1.3.17, the sub-classifications (or classes) of total cash receipts and payments which will be disclosed in accordance with Cash Basis IPSAS 1.3.12 and 1.3.14 are a matter of professional judgment. Total cash receipts may be classified to, for example, separately identify cash receipts from: taxation or appropriation; grants and donations; borrowings; proceeds from the disposal of property, plant and equipment; and other ongoing service delivery and trading activities. Total cash payments may be classified to, for example, separately identify cash payments in respect of: ongoing service delivery activities including transfers to constituents or other governments or entities; debt reduction programs; acquisitions of property, plant and equipment; and any trading activities. Alternative presentations are also possible. For example, total cash receipts may be classified by reference to their source and cash payments may be sub-classified by reference to either the nature of the payments or their function or program within the entity, as appropriate.

Treatment of payments by third parties on behalf of the entity

Where, during a reporting period, a third party directly settles the obligations of an entity or purchases goods and services for the benefit of the entity, the entity should disclose this in separate columns on the face of the statement of cash receipts and payments (cf. Cash Basis IPSAS 1.3.24). It must distinguish between total payments:

(a) Made by third parties which are part of the economic entity to which the reporting entity belongs

(b) Made by third parties which are not part of the economic entity to which the reporting entity belongs

A sub-classification of the sources and uses of total payments using a classification basis appropriate to the entity's operations must also be shown separately in each case.

Disclosures in the notes

Cash Basis IPSAS 1.3.30 states that the notes to the financial statements of an entity using the Cash Basis IPSAS should:

(a) Present information about the basis of preparation of the financial statements and the specific accounting policies selected and applied for significant transactions and other events

(b) Provide additional information which is not presented on the face of the financial statements but is necessary for a fair presentation of the entity's cash receipts, cash payments and cash balances

Cash Basis IPSAS 1.4.1 provides for the general purpose financial statements to be presented at least annually. If the reporting date changes and financial statements are presented for a period other than one year, this must be disclosed. IPSAS 1.4.4 states the financial statements should be issued within six months of the reporting date. However, the IPSASB strongly encourage a timeframe of no more than three months.

According to Cash Basis IPSAS 1.4.5, an entity should disclose the date when the financial statements were authorized for issue and who gave that authorization.

Consolidated financial statements

A controlling entity should issue consolidated financial statements which consolidate all controlled entities, foreign and domestic (cf. IPSAS 1.6.5), other than controlled entities operating under severe external long-term restrictions which prevent the controlling entity from benefiting from its activities.

Cash Basis IPSAS 1.6.7 provides that a controlling entity that is a wholly owned controlled entity does not have to present consolidated financial statements provided users of such financial statements are unlikely to exist or their information needs are met by the controlling entity's consolidated financial statements.

According to Cash Basis IPSAS 1.6.8, the same applies to a controlling entity that is virtually wholly owned, provided the controlling entity obtains the approval of the owners of the minority interest.

Cash Basis IPSAS 1.6.16 sets out this **procedure for consolidation**:

1. Cash balances and cash transactions between entities within the economic entity should be eliminated in full.
2. When the financial statements used in a consolidation are drawn up to different reporting dates, adjustments should be made for the effects of significant cash transactions that have occurred between those dates and the date of the controlling entity's financial statements.
3. Consolidated financial statements should be prepared using uniform accounting policies for like cash transactions.

The aim of consolidation is to reflect only transactions between the consolidating entity and other entities external to it, thus preventing double-counting of transactions.

Treatment of foreign currency transactions and foreign currency balances

Cash receipts and payments arising from transactions in a foreign currency should be recorded in an entity's reporting currency (cf. Cash Basis

IPSAS 1.7.2). To do this, the exchange rate between the reporting currency and the foreign currency is applied to the foreign currency at the date of the receipts and payments. By contrast, cash balances held in a foreign currency should be reported using the closing rate. The cash receipts and cash payments of a foreign controlled entity should be translated at the exchange rates between the reporting currency and the foreign currency at the dates of the receipts and payments (Cash Basis IPSAS 1.7.4). An entity should disclose the amount of exchange differences included as reconciling items between opening and closing cash balances for the period (cf. Cash Basis IPSAS 1.7.5).

Presentation of budget information in financial statements

An entity that makes publicly available its approved budget(s) must present a comparison of the budget amounts and actual amounts either as a separate additional financial statement or as additional budget columns in the statement of cash receipts and payments currently presented in accordance with the Cash Basis IPSAS (cf. Cash Basis IPSAS 1.9.8).

An entity must present a comparison of budget and actual amounts as additional budget columns in the statement of cash receipts and payments only where the financial statements and the budget are prepared on a comparable basis. Otherwise a reconciliation statement is required (cf. Cash Basis IPSAS 1.9.17).

The comparison of budget and actual amounts must present separately for each level of legislative oversight (cf. Cash Basis IPSAS 1.9.8):

(a)   The original and final budget amounts

(b)   The actual amounts on a comparable basis

(c)   An entity must present by way of note disclosure in the financial statements an explanation of material differences between the budget and actual amounts unless such explanations are published in other public documents related to the financial statements. Reference must be made to these documents in the note disclosure.

Treatment of external assistance

External assistance means all official resources which the recipient can use or otherwise benefit from in pursuit of its objectives (cf. Cash Basis IPSAS 1.10.1). Official resources mean all loans, grants, technical assistance, guarantees or other assistance provided or committed under a binding agreement by multilateral or bilateral external assistance agencies or by a government. They do not include assistance within one nation.

The entity should disclose separately on the face of the statement of cash receipts and payments, total external assistance received in cash during the period (cf. Cash Basis IPSAS 1.10.8).

The entity should disclose separately, either on the face of the statement of cash receipts and payments or in the notes to the financial statements, total external assistance paid by third parties during the period (cf. Cash Basis IPSAS 1.10.9). External assistance is provided either to settle an obligation of the entity or to purchase goods and services for the benefit of the entity. Total payments made by third parties, broken down into those which are and which are not part of the economic entity to which the reporting entity belongs, must be presented (cf. Cash Basis IPSAS 1.10.9). These disclosures should only be made when, during the reporting period, the entity has been formally advised by the third party or the recipient that such payment has been made, or has otherwise verified the payment.

Where external assistance is received from more than one source, the significant classes of sources of assistance should be disclosed separately, either on the face of the statement of cash receipts and payments or in the notes to the financial statements (cf. Cash Basis IPSAS 1.10.10).

Where external assistance is received in the form of loans and grants, the total amount received during the period as loans and the total amount received as grants should be shown separately, either on the face of the statement of cash receipts and payments or in the notes to the financial statements (cf. Cash Basis IPSAS 1.10.11).

Overview – part 2:

Part 2 sets out some encouraged additional disclosures. These include:

- An assessment of the entity's ability to continue as a going concern and, where necessary, material uncertainties (cf. Cash Basis IPSAS 2.1.3).
- Disclosures on the nature and amount of each extraordinary item, either on the face of the statement of cash receipts and payments, or in other financial statements or in the notes to the financial statements (cf. Cash Basis IPSAS 2.1.6).

Other additional (recommended) disclosures relate primarily to the notes to the financial statements (cf. Cash Basis IPSAS 2.1.15 et seq.)

Effective date

For part 1, section 1.1-1.7: periods beginning on or after 1 January 2004.

For part 1, section 1.9 and 1.10: periods beginning on or after 1 January 2009.

Further reading

Adam, Berit, Internationale Rechnungslegungsstandards für die öffentliche Verwaltung (IPSAS) – Eine kritische Analyse unter besonderer Berücksichtigung ihrer Anwendbarkeit in Deutschland, Frankfurt am Main 2004, also as a dissertation, Deutsche Hochschule für Verwaltungswissenschaften Speyer 2003

Bergmann, Andreas, Key Findings zum Projekt, in: Rechnungslegungsstandards für Kantone und Gemeinden im Rahmen von IPSAS (International Public Sector Accounting Standards), edited by Andreas Bergmann and Andreas Gamper, Zurich 2004, pages 1-8

Bergmann, Andreas and Andreas Gamper, Chancen und Gefahren der Anwendung von IPSAS: Erfahrungen anhand eines Pilotprojektes mit der Stadt Kloten, in: Der Schweizer Treuhänder, 2004, volume 8, pages 618-624

Bergmann, Andreas and Andreas Gamper, Rechnungslegungsstandards für Kantone und Gemeinden im Rahmen von IPSAS (International Public Sector Accounting Standards), Zurich 2004

Bergmann, Andreas, Public Sector Financial Management, Harlow, Essex 2009

Cardinaux, Pierre-Alain and Sandrine Lambert, Les Administrations Publiques face aux enjeux des normes IPSAS, L'exemple des Transports publiques de Genève, in: Der Schweizer Treuhänder, 2007, volume 9, pages 630-635

Chan, James L., Government Accounting: An Assessment of Theory, Purposes and Standards, in: Public Money & Management, 2003, volume 23, pages 13-20

Chan, James L., Une revolution mondiale dans la comptabilite public? Une analyse des IPSAS et quelques recommendations, in: Revue française de comptabilité, January 2004, pp. 27-31

Chan, James L., IPSAS and Government Accounting Reform in Developing Countries, in: Accounting Reform in the Public Sector: Mimicry, Fad or Necessity, edited by Evelyne Lande and Jean-Claude Scheid, Paris 2006, pp. 31-42

Cheney, Glenn, IFAC tackles governmental social policy obligations, in: Accounting Today, 2005, volume 19, page 3

Cheney, Glenn, IPSASB proposes standard on non-exchange revenue, in: Accounting Today, 2006, volume 20, page 3

Cheney, Glenn, United Nations adopts full accrual accounting, in: Accounting Today, 2006, volume 20, pages 14-16

Davis, Annette, Accounting for social benefits, in: Chartered Accountants Journal, 2008, volume 87, pages 54-55

Davis, Annette, The IPSASB – developing high quality accounting standards, in: Chartered Accountants Journal, 2008, volume 87, pages 23-24

Hughes, Jesse W., Transitioning from Current Basis to Full Accrual Basis of Accounting for Governments in Developing Countries, in: Journal of Government Financial Management, 2007, volume 56, pages 20-26

Kussmaul, Heinz and Jörg Henkes, § 43 Öffentliche Verwaltung (Internationnal Public Sector Accounting Standards – IPSAS), in: Haufe IFRS commentary, edited by Norbert Lüdenbach and Wolf-Dieter Hoffmann, 6th edition, Freiburg i. Br. 2008, pages 2333-2373

Laughlin, Richard, A Conceptual Framework for Accounting for Public-Benefit Entities, in: Public Money & Management, 2008, volume 28, pages 247-254

Lüder, Klaus, Internationale Standards für das öffentliche Rechnungswesen: Entwicklungsstand und Anwendungsperspektiven, in: Finanzpolitik und Finanzkontrolle: Partner für Veränderung, Gedächtnisschrift für Udo Müller, edited by Manfred Eibelshäuser, Baden-Baden 2002, pages 151-166

Lüder, Klaus, Globalisierung und transnationale Entwickungen des öffentlichen Rechnungswesens, in: Globale und monetäre Ökonomie, Festschrift für Dieter Duwendag, edited by Hermann Knödler and Michael H. Stierle, Heidelberg 2003, pages 407-418

Lüder, Klaus, Internationale Harmonisierung des öffentlichen Rechnungs-wesens?, in: Öffentliche Verwaltung und Nonprofit-Organisationen, Festschrift für Reinbert Schauer, edited by Ernst-Bernd Blümle et. al., Vienna 2003, pages 341-357

Lüder, Klaus, Zur Reform des öffentlichen Rechnungswesens in Europa, in: WPg, 2004, special volume, pages 11-18

Mackintosh, Ian, Aus der Arbeit des IFAC Public Sector Committee, in: Reform der Rechnungslegung der öffentlichen Verwaltung, Die Wirtschaftsprüfung – special volume, 2004, pages 3-7

Müller-Marqués Berger, Thomas, Verpflichtungen aus Sozialpolitik und deren bilanzielle Abbildung, Das Standards-Project des IFAC Public Sector Committee, in: Reform der Rechnungslegung der öffentlichen Verwaltung, Die Wirtschaftsprüfung – special volume, pages 41-49

Müller-Marqués Berger, Thomas and Markus Häfele, Leistungen an Arbeitnehmer: Entwurf eines IPSAS, in: Die Wirtschaftsprüfung, 2007, pages 643-646

Pina, Vicente and Lourdes Torres, Accounting Developments of Spanish Local Governments: An International Comparison, in: Journal of Public Budgeting, Accounting & Financial Management, 2002, volume 14, pages 619-654

Pina, Vicente and Lourdes Torres, Reshaping Public Sector Accounting: An International Comparative View, in: Canadian Journal of Administrative Sciences, 2003, volume 20, pages 334-350

Points, Ronald J. and Simon Bradbury, International Public Sector Accounting Standards, in: Journal of Government Financial Management, 2001, volume 50, pages 48-52

Sanderson, Ian and Frans van Schaik, Taking Control, in: Accountancy, 2008, volume 142, pages 86-87

Sanderson, Ian and Frans Van Schaik, Public Sector Accounting Standards: Strengthening accountability and improving governance, in: Accountancy Ireland, 2008, volume 40, pages 22-24

Schauer, Reinbert, International Public Sector Accounting Standards (IPSAS) – Notwendigkeit für eine Reform des öffentlichen Rechnungswesens?, in: Birgit Feldbauer-Durstmüller, Reinhard Schwarz and Bernhard Wimmer (eds.), Handbuch Controlling und Consulting, Festschrift für Harald Stiegler, Vienna 2005, pages 591-612

Schauer, Reinbert, Anhang: International Public Sector Accounting Standards (IPSAS), in: Die „Kommunale Doppik", Theoretische und praktische Überlegungen zur Neuorganisation des kommunalen Rechnungswesens im Lichte internationaler Erfahrungen, conference at Johannes Kepler University Linz, seminar documents, edited by Reinbert Schauer, Linz 2007, pages 145-162

Schedler, Kuno and Bernhard Knechtenhofer, IPSAS als möglicher Leitfaden für aktuelle Entwicklungen in der Rechnungslegung öffentlicher Gemeinwesen in der Schweiz, in: Öffentliche Verwaltung und Nonprofit-Organisationen, Festschrift für Reinbert Schauer, Vienna 2003, pages 543-560

Schedler, Kuno and Bernhard Knechtenhofer, IPSAS in der Praxisanwendung – mehr Richtlinie als Standard?, in: Controlling und Performance Management im Öffentlichen Sektor, Ein Handbuch, edited by Martin Brüggemeier, Reinbert Schauer, Kuno Schedler, Berne, Stuttgart, Vienna 2007, pages 299-307

Schreyer, Michaele, Accounting in the Public Sector – European Commission Perspectives –, in: Reform der Rechnungslegung der öffentlichen Verwaltung, Die Wirtschaftsprüfung – special volume, pages 7-11

Srocke, Isabell, Konzernrechnungslegung in Gebietskörperschaften unter Berücksichtigung von HGB, IAS/IFRS und IPSAS, Düsseldorf 2004, also a dissertation for Hamburger Universität für Wirtschaft und Politik 2003

Streim, Hannes, Rechnungslegung von Gebietskörperschaften – HGB versus IPSAS, in: Controlling und Performance Management im Öffentlichen Sektor, Ein Handbuch, edited by Martin Brüggemeier, Reinbert Schauer, Kuno Schedler, Berne, Stuttgart, Vienna 2007, pages 291-298

Utelli, Christophe and Patrick Hauri, Finanzinstrumente unter IPSAS, Was erwartet den öffentlichen Sektor mit der Umstellung auf IPSAS 15?, in: Der Schweizer Treuhänder, 2006, 1-2, pages 56-60

Viehweger, Cathérine, Bilanzielle Behandlung von gesellschaftlichen Verpflichtungen des öffentlichen Sektors, in: Die Zukunft des Öffentlichen Rechnungswesens, Reformtendenzen und internationale Entwicklungen, edited by Heinz Bolsenkötter, Baden-Baden 2007, pages 193-208

Viehweger, Cathérine, Wertminderungen von Zahlungsmittel generierenden Vermögenswerten – Entwurf eines IPSAS –, in: Die Wirtschaftsprüfung, 2007, volume 6, pages 246-248

Vogelpoth, Norbert, Vergleich der IPSAS mit den deutschen Rechnungslegungsgrundsätzen für den öffentlichen Bereich, in: Reform der Rechnungslegung der öffentlichen Verwaltung, Die Wirtschaftsprüfung – special volume, 2004, pages 23-40

Vogelpoth, Norbert, Haushaltsplanung und internationale Rechnungslegung, in: Controlling und Performance Management im Öffentlichen Sektor, Ein Handbuch, edited by Martin Brüggemeier, Reinbert Schauer, Kuno Schedler, Berne, Stuttgart, Vienna 2007, pages 263-270

Vogelpoth, Norbert and Andreas Dörschell, Internationale Rechnungslegungsstandards für öffentliche Verwaltungen, das Standards-Project des IFAC Public Sector Commitee, in: Die Wirtschaftsprüfung, 2001, volume 14-15, pages 752-762

Vogelpoth, Norbert, Andreas Dörschell and Cathérine Viehweger, Die Bilanzierung und Bewertung von Sachanlagevermögen nach den International Public Sector Accounting Standards, in: Die Wirtschaftsprüfung, 2002, volume 24, pages 1360-1371

Vogelpoth, Norbert, Andreas Dörschell and Cathérine Viehweger, Rechnungslegung nach IPSAS – Aktuelle Entwicklungen, in: Die Wirtschaftsprüfung, 2007, pages 1000-1011

Wirtz, Holger, Grundsätze ordnungsmäßiger öffentlicher Buchführung, dissertation, University of Duisburg-Essen, Berlin 2008